JOHN CAIRNEY, 'The Man Who Played Robert Burns', is an actor, writer, lecturer, recitalist, director and theatre consultant, football fan and most recently, has exhibited as a painter. He graduated in drama in 1953 from the Glasgow College of Drama and gained an MLitt from Glasgow University for *A History of Solo Theatre* in 1989.

In a career that has spanned more than half a century, John Cairney has played in every media – theatre, radio, television and film. He has performed on stages as various as London's West End to the garden room of a millionaire's home in Texas, and before every kind of audience from Britain's royal family to a hall full of shipyard workers out on strike in Glasgow. His films include *Jason and the Argonauts, Victim* and *A Night to Remember.*

Having played RLS in solo performance, Cairney developed a fascination with the many-faceted personality of his subject. Dr Cairney's PhD, gained from Victoria University, Wellington in 1994, dealt with the theatricality of RLS and concentrated on the Stevenson plays. Fortunate to have a career that takes him on tour, John Cairney has been able to fuel his interest in Stevenson and has visited every RLS site around the world. He now lives in the South Pacific, making his home in Auckland with his New Zealand wife, Alannah O'Sullivan.

By the same author:

A Moment White, 1986 (Outram Press)
The Man Who Played Robert Burns, 1987 (Mainstream)
East End to West End, 1988 (Mainstream)
Worlds Apart, 1991 (Mainstream)
A Year Out in New Zealand, 1993 (Tandem Press)
A Scottish Football Hall of Fame, 1998 (Mainstream)
On the Trail of Robert Burns, 2000 (Luath Press)
The Luath Burns Companion, 2001 (Luath Press)
Solo Performers, 1770–2000: An International Registry, 2001 (McFarland)
Immortal Memories, 2003 (Luath Press)
The Quest for Charles Rennie Mackintosh, 2004 (Luath Press)
Heroes Are Forever, 2005 (Mainstream)
Glasgow By the Way, But 2006 (Luath Press)

The Quest for
Robert Louis Stevenson

JOHN CAIRNEY

Luath Press Limited

EDINBURGH

www.luath.co.uk

First published 2004
First paperback edition published 2007

The paper used in this book is recyclable.
It is made from low-chlorine pulps produced in a
low-emission manner from renewable forests.

Printed and bound by
Bookmarque, Croydon
Typeset in 10.5 point Sabon

ISBN (10) 1-84282-085-0
ISBN (13) 978-1-8-4282085-8

*This volume is dedicated to Alanna Knight
who, in Aberdeen, sometime in 1973,
first suggested that I play Robert Louis Stevenson
in the theatre. It all started from there.*

Contents

Acknowledgements

IF ALANNA KNIGHT started me off with Stevenson in the theatre, Professor Jan McDonald of Glasgow University pointed me towards Stevenson in the study. Emeritus Professor Ian A Gordon of Victoria University at Wellington, New Zealand, Professor George D Bryan of the University of Vermont and Dr David Daiches of Edinburgh awakened me to the mind of Stevenson. For the facts of his life, especially through the letters, I could look no further than Dr Ernest J Mehew of London, the supreme Stevenson authority of our time, and likewise I owe much to the unimpeachable authority of Stevenson scholars such as Roger Swearingham, Jenni Calder and Alan Sandison, and the work of JC Furnas, Nicholas Rankin, Ian Bell, Gavin Bell, Richard Woodhead, Karen Steele and particularly Frank McLynn whose 1993 book proved an invaluable source.

Further research opportunities were made available to me by following libraries: the Mitchell Library, Glasgow; the British Library, London; New York Public Library; Special Collections at Columbia University; the Beineke Collection at Yale University; the Widener Collection at Harvard University and the libraries of Glasgow and Auckland Universities; and to librarians, Margaret Furlong and Donald Kerr in Auckland for extra assistance. Thanks are also due to Ian A Nimmo and the Robert Louis Stevenson Club in Edinburgh, and to the late John Cargill Thompson.

Thanks are also due to Rosemary Smith and Maureen Bianchini in Monterey. My gratitude for unstinting hospitality goes to Michael Westcott in Edinburgh, Clare Brotherwood in Maidenhead, Berkshire, the Baldwins in New York, the Joneses in Cleveland, the Turnbows in Fort Worth, the Parmelees in San Francisco, Lilian Cunningham in Honolulu, the Neales in Sydney, and the Connell family in Wellington. Special thanks to Tifai Tagiilima and Rex Maughan in Apia and to Seutatia Mata'utia Pene Solomona of the Faculty of Education at the National University of Samoa.

I am indebted to Elaine Greig of the Edinburgh Writers' Museum for her advice and for her permission to reproduce images from the Museum's Stevenson archive, and to Dr Alan Marchbank for guidance on Stevenson points. As always, I must acknowledge the encouragement and inspiration given by my publisher, Gavin MacDougall, and the staff at Luath Press.

Finally, I must thank my daughters, Jennifer, Alison, Lesley and Jane for the open houses they gave me in Los Angeles, Glasgow, Newcastle and Dunfermline, and my patient wife, Alannah O'Sullivan, who granted me generous leave of absence so that I might make my way along the long, long trail that finally led me to RLS. As my son, Jonathan said, 'I don't know how you do it, Daddy.' Then he put me in my place by adding, 'At your age.'

Introduction

It is a singular thing that I should live here in the South Seas, under conditions so new and striking, yet my imagination should continually inhabit that old, cold huddle of grey hills from which I came so long ago; those Pentland Hills, and the Lammermuirs, and further still, the whole of that Border country, where my Elliott ancestors had shaken a spear in the debatable land.

I have come so far, yet the sights and sounds of my youth still pursue me, and it is Edinburgh, that venerable city I still think of as home. Yet I know, even as I stand here now, I shall never see home again. Here I am until I die. The word is out, the doom is written, and I bow my head to the romance of my own destiny.

I CAME TO ROBERT LOUIS STEVENSON through the theatre as a part to be played. I got to know him initially through a playscript written by Alanna Knight that was as faithful as possible to his own words and I became aware that beneath the patina of literary elegance was a character of steely resolve and determination. I found the best way to perform him was to let him speak for himself. As far as possible, I have done the same in this book.

I am writing this in New Zealand, where I now live. Through my study window I can see pohutakawa, kowhai, palm and rata trees. All around, a vibrant palette of exotic colour set against every imaginable shade of green tells me unequivocally that I am not in Scotland. I well understand the pull our dreich old native country had on Stevenson, however much he adored the lush drama of his Samoan setting. And, had it not been for an early New Zealand connection, he might never have gone there at all – might never have played that great, iconic role, the Tusitala of the South Seas, an image that is as compelling today as it was in Victorian times.

William Seed, a distant relative of the Stevensons and an Inspector for the Crown Colony of New Zealand's Marine and Customs, was originally responsible for intriguing him with his descriptions of the South Seas islands. In 1875 Seed visited Edinburgh and stayed with the family at Heriot Row in order to discuss with Thomas Stevenson the engineering challenges involved in building a ring of lighthouses round the New Zealand coast.

Louis wrote to Fanny Sitwell:

> Awfully nice man here tonight. Public servant – New Zealand – telling us all about the South Seas Islands till I was sick with a desire to go there; beautiful places, green forever; perfect climate; perfect shapes of men and women, with red flowers in their hair; and nothing to do but to study oratory and etiquette, sit in the sun and pick up fruits as they fall; absolute balm for the weary...

The 'seed' had fallen on fertile ground, though it took fifteen years to germinate. Writing from Sydney in 1890 (referring to Samoa as the Navigator Islands, as they were then called), he recalled,

> ... in '74 or 5 there came to stay with my father and mother in Edinburgh, a certain Mr Seed, a prime minister or something in New Zealand. He spotted what my complaint was; told me I had no business to stay in Europe; that I should find... all that was good for me in the Navigator Islands; sat up till four in the morning persuading me, demolishing all my scruples. And I resisted; I refused to go so far from my father and mother. O, it was virtuous, and O, wasn't it silly? And now in 1890, I (or what is left of me) go at last to the Navigator Islands.

Belle Strong visited Seed shortly after her stepfather's death, bringing gifts of some desirable personal memorabilia – his flageolet, tartan plaid and favourite velvet jacket. As it happens, through all the years I played RLS on stage I wore a Victorian velvet jacket. Alanna Knight had discovered it in a trunk in her attic. With black braid round the pockets and collar and four cloth-covered buttons, it was just the sort of jacket Stevenson so often wore. It seems that one of Alanna's mother's friends had actually been a chambermaid at 17 Heriot Row in the decade after the Stevensons sold it. I know that it would be a pretty long shot that this jacket might have belonged to RLS, but whenever I wore it on stage, I always felt that it was his – it helped me 'become' him.

In working with RLS as a character on the page and on the stage, I have developed my own opinion of him. Throughout his life he adjusted himself, chameleon-like as an actor, to each new scene. He said, 'There is no foreign land. It is the traveller only that is foreign' and protested his Scottishness to the last – 'I am a Scotsman, touch me and you will find a thistle.' Yet it seems to me that nowhere was he a greater stranger than in Scotland itself.

To set him before the reader as I see him, I have put in my own tuppence-worth here and there. Sometimes, in order to get to the essential truth of a situation, it is necessary to imagine it. We can feel a thing is right even when we have no direct factual evidence to support our intuition. It does not make for the highest scholarship, but it makes a better story. Every life is more than a dry accretion of verifiable facts. Stevenson himself said:

> I like biography far better than fiction myself. You have your little handful of facts, little bits of a puzzle, and you sit and think, and fit 'em together this way and that, and get up and throw them down and say 'damn' and go for a walk, and it's real soothing, and when it's done it gives an idea of finish to the writer that is very peaceful. Of course, it's not really so finished as quite a rotten novel; it always has, and must have the incurable illogicalities of life about it... still, that's where the fun comes in.

Some years ago on a visit to Edinburgh I went to see Alan and Maria Finlayson, a theatrical couple whose fifth child, Orlando, had been born only a week previously. Maria carried the sleeping infant with her as she showed me round their house.

Eventually we reached a small back bedroom. Maria pointed to the carpet and said, 'Orlando was born here.'

'On the carpet?'

'On the carpet!' she confirmed, with a beam.

I walked over to the window. Through the rain-spattered panes everything in sight was dank and cheerless. Even so, my mood was lifted at the thought of the new life. I must confess, I wasn't thinking of little Orlando Finlayson. I was thinking of another baby, born at 8 Howard Place over 150 years before.

To believe in immortality is one thing,
but it is first needful to believe in life.
OLD MORTALITY

CHAPTER ONE

Grit and Grace

If you are going to make a book end badly,
it must end badly from the beginning.
RLS IN A LETTER TO JAMES BARRIE

ROBERT LOUIS STEVENSON was a child of Edinburgh's New Town. It still thought of itself as new, even though it was already into stately middle age by the time he was born. The New Town was a bastion of bourgeois rectitude – middle-class and middle of the road and taking care at all times to give the right impression. Edinburgh is the key to our subject's life-long obsession with duality. The city has two faces, a division which is less topographical than social. The huddled Old Town on the hill below the ancient castle looks north to the set squares and prim rectangles of the New Town. The wide boulevard of Princes Street, a once beautiful Georgian lady, who for the last fifty years has been ravaged by commercial bandits, is the 'No Man's Land' between the two sets of Edinburgh citizenry.

If we are to understand Stevenson, we must first understand his Janus-like city. His psyche parallels its dichotomy, the contradictions and anomalies of his personality echoing those of the streets, wynds and alleyways that surrounded him in his formative years. The effect of his native city was tenacious. In Samoa, he yearned for 'the hills of home' – hills that might not have been the Pentlands, but rather, Heriot Row to Stockbridge, or Leith Walk to Calton Hill. Edinburgh retains a quasi-Englishness that sits like a genteel antimacassar on the neolithic pile they call Arthur's Seat, and so it should be no surprise that its famous son has sometimes been called Scotland's best writer of English prose. The two-sided city and its two-faced populace are apt metaphors for the man himself. It is no accident that Stevenson's keyword, *duality*, is closely related to hypocrisy, duplicity, artifice, pretence and other pejorative terms indicating the sham and the false. He was never afraid to pretend, if it suited his book, and a tendency to the histrionic was there from the start.

This bipartite, not to say multi-faceted faculty, permeated his whole life and explains why he seemed to be giving a performance at every stage. He was always 'on', as actors say, and the 'tuppence-coloured' side of him far outweighed the 'penny plain'. It was this element in his character that caused him to be labelled so often as a *poseur*, especially during his Edinburgh youth and early London days. He could *be* one person, yet *play* another. His very theatricality gave him an understanding of the dual personality in himself and this was the crucial insight that enabled him to create Dr Jekyll *and* Mr Hyde, and to present each brilliantly as a facet of the other.

In Stevenson's unique expression of duality, he was only being true to his Edinburgh genesis – Scots and English, up and down, profligate and miserly, practical and impractical. Within him, his Stevenson blood was continually at war with his Balfour blood.

The stream of his paternal ancestry is a tributary of the Clyde rather than the Forth. James Stevenson, the first ancestor he claimed, was a farmer at Neilston, near Glasgow. His son Robert was a maltster in Glasgow, as was *his* son, who then had two sons himself, Hugh and Alan, both merchants. As a young man Hugh went to the West Indies to look after business interests there, which included the ownership of St Kitt's in the Leeward Islands. Alan stayed in Glasgow and in 1772 married Jean Lillie, whose father was the Deacon of Wrights. It would seem that their marriage had to be arranged rather hurriedly.

As Stevenson liked to say, 'With these two brothers, my story begins...' It appears that Hugh was swindled out of the family money and property by a dishonest agent in Trinidad, and in proper Glasgow fashion he sent for his brother to help him sort out the rascal. Unfortunately both of them, 'drenched by the pernicious dews of the Tropics', died while pursuing their quarry from island to island: Hugh at Tobago and, a month later, Alan, drowned, at St Kitt's. (*Treasure Island* owes much to this family lore.) Then, to make matters worse, Mr Lillie's business failed, and he died. His daughter was left widowed, fatherless, penniless and with a son, another Robert Stevenson, aged two. She subsequently married a James Hogg but their union did not last long. By 1787 she and her son, now aged fifteen, moved from Glasgow to Edinburgh where she met and married a successful merchant Tom Smith (whose father, a Broughty Ferry fisherman, had also drowned, in Dundee harbour). Jean had intended Robert for the manse but instead he became an apprentice to his step-father, the 'lamp and oil man', who, at this time, had just been appointed Engineer to the newly-formed Board of Northern Lighthouses. Robert not only followed in his footsteps, but married Tom Smith's daughter. And so a great line of engineers was begun.

Robert Stevenson went on to build the famous Bell Rock Lighthouse and father three sons, Alan, David and Thomas, all civil engineers. (Alan, who built the equally famous lighthouse at Skerryvore, was cursed with a poor constitution; after his early retirement he became a religious recluse.)

Not one of the Stevenson lighthouse engineers registered patents on their innovations, although this was standard practice. They apparently regarded their engineering talents as God-given and intended to be shared with their fellow men. This altruistic spirit was their hallmark. As Stevenson put it:

I have often thought that to find a family to compare with ours in the promise of immortal memory we must go back to the Egyptian Pharaohs – upon so many reefs and forelands that not very elegant name of Stevenson is engraved with a pen of iron upon granite... Whenever I smell salt water I know I am not far from the works of my ancestors... and when the lights come on at sundown along the shores of Scotland, I am proud to think they burn more brightly for the genius of my father.

In 1846, aged twenty-eight, Tom Stevenson became a partner in the family business and two years later he married the nineteen-year-old Margaret Isabella Balfour, a tall, slim minister's daughter, whom he had met on a train. In 1850 she gave birth to their only child, whom the world was to know as RLS.

He was born at his parents' first home, 8 Howard Place, in a Georgian terrace near Canonmills, and he was christened there, after the Scottish fashion, by his own grandfather, the Reverend Lewis Balfour. He was named, as was the tradition, after his paternal and maternal grandfathers – Robert Lewis Balfour Stevenson. He was to Frenchify the 'Lewis' to Louis in his university years (although he was never 'Loo-ee': the family always pronounced it in the Scots way – 'Loo-iss'). At the age of eighteen, he was to drop the 'Balfour', but young Louis loved his old grandfather, the venerable sage of Colinton,

one of the last to speak broad Scots and still be a gentleman... I often wonder what I have inherited from this old minister... try as I please, I cannot join myself on with the reverend doctor... and, no doubt, even as I write the phrase, he moves in my blood and whispers to me, and sits efficient in the very knot and centre of my being.

The distaff side of the Stevenson family, the Balfours, boasted several gentlemen of the cloth in a gentrified line which went all the way back to Flodden and before. Stevenson described this side of his family as 'being of good provincial stock... related to many of the so-called good families of Scotland'. James Balfour, 'of the long beard', Minister at Guthrie and later the East Kirk of St Giles, was the first Balfour to take orders. His son Andrew, also a minister, at Kirknewton, died at thirty-seven leaving three children one of whom rose to become an advocate and principal Clerk of Session in 1649. His son and namesake, James, became a successful businessman with a soap factory and glass works in Leith, gained the monopoly for the manufacture of gunpowder, lost everything in the doomed

Darien Scheme of 1698 and died, broke, at the age of fifty. (At one time he had been wealthy enough to lend King Charles II the sum of ten thousand pounds. Needless to say, the Merry Monarch neglected to repay it.)

His heir, the next James Balfour, intended to seek his fortune abroad. But before going away he attended a wedding in Hamilton and came back to Edinburgh with a bride of his own, his cousin, Louisa Hamilton, the 'Fair Flower of Clydesdale', and a new determination to face out his future in Scotland. Lucky in love, he was also lucky in life. On the Union of the Parliaments in 1707 some of the Darien money was repaid and with his share he bought Pilrig House, an estate in the countryside between Edinburgh and Leith, where he and his wife lived happily ever after as the Laird of Pilrig and his Lady.

The young Stevenson loved hearing these family tales – 'tradition whispered to me in my childhood...' He had Balfour 'eyes with the gypsy light behind' and the distinctive Balfour profile.

Seventeen children were born to Louisa. Thirteen survived. James, the oldest son and second Laird of Pilrig, became a distinguished lawyer who was not afraid to cross swords with the great David Hume. Indeed, he defeated Hume to gain the Chair of Moral Philosophy at Edinburgh University, and later held the Chair of Nature and Nations until his death in 1795, in his ninetieth year.

The Borders strain was brought into the family by Professor Balfour's marriage to Cecilia Elphinstone, daughter of Sir John Elphinstone of Logie whose wife Mary Elliot was the daughter of Sir Gilbert Elliot of Minto, later Lord Minto. Through this connection RLS could claim kinship to Sir Walter Scott, and going even further back, to Rob Roy MacGregor. At the time when the clan was proscribed, Rob Roy was a MacGregor by night and a Stevenson by day – an early instance of that thematic duality.

The third Laird of Pilrig, John Balfour, was one of the first residents of the brand-new Princes Street. His second son, Thomas, was the father of Stevenson's future biographer, Graham Balfour. His third son, Lewis, 'an amiable and clever young man' became the minister at Sorn in Ayrshire and the husband of Henrietta Scott Smith, a great beauty and daughter of the Reverend Dr Smith of Galston. In 1823 Lewis Balfour was called to the parish of Colinton south of Edinburgh. Chronic chest trouble did not prevent his fathering thirteen children and heading his family with patriarchal authority. His youngest child, Margaret, inherited the family tendency to pulmonary weakness and she passed it on to her only son, who wrote:

I know not what is more strange, that I should carry about with me some fibres of a minister-grandfather, or, that in him, as he sat in his cool study, there was an aboriginal frisking in the blood that was not his, or that tree-top instincts lying dormant in his mind awoke to gambol in the brain of an old divine.

There you have the essence of heredity, that atavistic chain that stretches back from everyone to Adam. We are the aggregate of everything that has gone into us, or, as Stevenson put it, 'Our conscious years are but a moment in the elements that built us'. In a letter to Henry James in 1888, he commented: 'I am one of the few people in the world who do not forget their own lives.' This preoccupation remained with him throughout his life and he touched on it in a letter to Sir Herbert Maxwell written only two days before he died: 'I see like a vision the youth of my father and his father before him and the whole stream of lives flowing down with the sound of laughter and tears.'

'RLS' was the merging of Stevenson grit and Balfour grace. Both elements were strikingly apparent as he grew to manhood. He was always pulled between the opposites his parents represented. To his father the teapot was always half empty and to his mother, it was always half full. Though he always joked that he had his father's legs and would always fall on his feet, he also had his mother's Balfour chest, and for that reason alone, there was always a question of whether he would survive the 'inspissated gloom' of his Edinburgh childhood home – not to mention the weather:

> In Edinburgh, the delicate die early. As a survivor, among
> bleak winds and plumping rain, I had sometimes been tempted
> to envy them their fate. For Edinburgh weather is raw and
> boisterous in winter, shifty and ungenial in summer and a
> downright meteorological purgatory in the spring.

In January 1853 the Stevensons moved to 1 (now 9) Inverleith
Terrace an imposing, north-facing property which was riddled with
damp and mildew. The worst affected room was the three-year-old
Smout's (so called because his father thought him 'such a wee smout
of a thing'). Nothing could have been worse for the little fellow.
His miseries began with an attack of croup, followed by whooping
cough. From this time on, there was never to be a year – except,
ironically, his last – when he did not have a catarrhal illness of some
kind. In a sense, the valetudinarian had been born at Inverleith Terrace. The father of the wasting man was the sickly boy.

> My ill-health principally chronicled itself by the terrible, long
> nights that I lay awake, troubled continually by a hacking,
> exhausting cough, and praying for sleep or morning from the
> bottom of my shaken little body.

The doctor became their most frequent visitor and it was on urgent medical advice that, in May 1857, the Stevensons moved house
again. Louis's second nanny, Mrs Hailey, had been discovered
drunk in a public house with her charge wrapped in a parcel behind
the bar. Alison Cunningham, his third nanny, (known as Cummy)
had just been appointed when the family moved into a splendid
New Town home facing south to Queen Street Gardens. Standing
outside 17 Heriot Row under the light of that famous street-lamp
and glancing up to the top floor where his nursery was, it is easy
to imagine the little figure of Stevenson as a boy being held up to
look out from the candle-lit window.

My recollections of the long nights when I was kept awake by the pain of coughing are only relieved by the tenderness of my nurse and second mother, (my first will not be jealous) Alison Cunningham. She was more patient than I can suppose of an angel... How well I remember her lifting me out of bed, carrying me to the window, and showing me one or two lit windows up in Queen Street across the dark belt of gardens; where also, we told each other, there might be sick little boys and their nurses waiting, like us, for the morning.

There is no denying that Cummy was devoted and caring, but her influence on the sensitive child could also have been dangerous. A doughty Calvinist with a fanatical hatred of Catholics, she succeeded in turning the imaginative six-year-old into a prayerful, hell-obsessed, Bible-biased, hymn-singing zealot.

I had an extreme terror of Hell, implanted in me, I suppose, by my good nurse, which used to haunt me terribly on stormy nights, when the wind had broken loose and was going about the town like a bedlamite...

She was forever reading to him from the Bible, preferring the parts that dealt with death, famines and disasters. She schooled him in the Shorter Catechism: 'What is the chief end of Man?' she would ask and the child would answer by rote, 'To glorify God and to enjoy him forever.'

He was constantly at prayer, praying for everybody and everything – even for his father's horse. He wondered if the family pets would go to Heaven, as they couldn't read the Bible. When his mother asked why he prayed so much, he didn't mention the constant terror of Hell inculcated in him by Cummy, but only said solemnly, 'You can never be good unless you pray.'

'How do you know that?'

'Because I've tried it.'

Cummy warned him about ghosts on the dark stairs and demons in every cupboard but she reserved her best for his Satanic Majesty, the Prince of Darkness. Didn't Lou know that the Devil was wandering through Auld Reekie in search of bad boys who didn't say their prayers? With thoughts like this to go to bed with, no wonder he couldn't sleep. On their walks together in Greyfriars Kirkyard he was encouraged to read the inscriptions on the tomb stones. The 'mort-safes' – graves ringed with an iron fence against the body-snatchers – impressed his imagination. Sometimes they went down into the Grassmarket where Cummy would point to the spot where the martyred Covenanters, those 'Sweet Singers', bade eloquent farewell to the sun, moon and stars, or died silent to the roll of Catholic drums.

Even nursery games were kirk-based. In the 'Church' game, his favourite, Louis would dress up as a minister in Cummy's cloak, stand on a chair, and with paper stuck in his collar as clerical bands, preach a sermon on hell-fire and damnation to anyone who would listen. This, the first of his 'characterisations' or 'performances', delighted Cummy and impressed his father. His mother was less amused and one of her friends was scandalised when, visiting with her own son, she heard Lou playing the 'minister'. In a fury, she pulled the paper bands from his neck and hauled her son away at once from that sacrilegious playroom.

The importance of Alison Cunningham in the formation of Stevenson's attitudes cannot be overestimated, even if he did recant most of them in later life. As Jenni Calder has pointed out, Stevenson, like certain other Victorian writers such as Dickens, Butler and Kingsley, carried a sense of guilt about his childhood.

But it is my view that the massive and overwhelming presence of Edinburgh itself provided his primary formative trauma. His only escape was into the ongoing theatre of his mind where he could play the part his dreams directed. His cousin Bob was also a dreamer:

Bob was three years older than I lived in a dream with his sisters and the Arabian Nights and less unfitted for the world than an angel. We lived together in a purely visionary state. We had our own countries. His was Nosingtonia, mine was Encyclopaedia. We ruled and made wars and inventions and we perpetually drew maps. We were never weary of dressing up. We drew and cut out and painted the figures for our pasteboard theatre. My toy theatre. This last was one of the dearest pleasures of my childhood and one I was loathe to relinquish. Indeed, it was one I followed in secret until I was fifteen or sixteen...

Sir James Barrie, who once described RLS as 'the most famous initials in the world', recognised the man-boy or 'Peter Pan' in him. Stevenson fitted Barrie's definition of genius – he always had 'that power to be a boy again at will'. As Andrew Lang said, Stevenson was 'not the only genius who has retained from childhood something more than its inspiration'.

As he was to prove over and over again, every experience counts, not least as raw material for stories. Out of Cummy's ghoulish fantasies, he would fashion stories such as 'The Body Snatcher' and 'The Story of Thrawn Janet', a short-story in Scots of extraordinary tautness and power and one of Stevenson's own favourites. The Balfour part of him recognised early that he was his own best copy. In a way, he created his own 'memory' of himself, and therefore it is perhaps between the lines that one should look for the real Robert Louis Stevenson.

As an only child, he was the centre of an adult world, a position he often childishly tried to maintain in adult life. He had little or no idea of what to expect when Cummy took him to the 'Beginners' School in Canonmills. The experience so unnerved him that he never went back. Goodness knows what the children there must have thought of him – a miniature skeleton with dark eyes and a tuft of fair hair, with the manner of an imperial prince and the speech of a cut-down adult. He later wrote in 'Child's Play':

Although the ways of children cross with those of their elders in a hundred places daily, they never go in the same direction nor so much as lie in the same element. So may telegraph wires intersect the line of the high road, or so might a landscape-painter and a bagman visit the same country and yet move in different worlds... Children think very much the same thoughts and dream the same dreams as bearded men and marriageable women... no one is more romantic... 'Art for Art's Sake' is their motto, and the doings of grown folk are only interesting as the raw material for play...

However perceptive, this was, of course, hindsight. As was this:

On the whole I have not much joy in remembering these early years. I was as much an egotist as I have ever been; I had feverish desire of consideration; I was ready to lie although more often wrongly accused of it, or rather, wrongfully punished for it, having lied unconsciously; I was sentimental, snivelling, goody, morbidly religious. I hope and I do believe I am a better man than I was as a child...

Nevertheless, it all had to be gone through again. In 1858 he was enrolled for an uneasy term of mornings only at Mr Henderson's Special School in India Street; it was eventually interrupted by a bout of gastric fever, probably brought on by sheer funk on the wee fellow's part. Even the short walk up the hill was too much for him, despite the after-breakfast training runs with his mother up and down Heriot Row. He had to stop at every stone step to take a rest:

I have three powerful impressions of my childhood: my sufferings when I was sick, my delight in convalescence at my grandfather's manse of Colinton, near Edinburgh, and the unnatural activity of my mind after I was in bed at night. As to the first, I suppose it is generally granted that none suffer like children from physical distress. We learn, as we grow older, a sort of courage under pain which marvellously lightens the endurance; we have made up our mind as to its existence as a part of life; but the spirit of the child is filled with dismay and indignation, and these pangs of the mind are often little less intolerable than the physical distress that cause them.

After these abortive educational experiments, he retreated into the familiar world of the nursery. He had taught himself to write in bold, large capitals even before he could read. When he was six his uncle, David Stevenson, had offered the family children gathered at the Colinton manse a prize of a pound for the best history of Moses. Young Louis dictated his version to his mother between November and December 1856. Complete with illustrations showing the Israelites in top hats and smoking pipes just like his father, he won. He followed this up with 'The Story of Joseph' and 'The American Travellers', again with his mother as adoring amanuensis. He had begun as an author.

'Travels in Perthshire' was started on the first of many family holidays in Bridge of Allan. Margaret Stevenson knew early on that it was, as she put it, 'the desire of his heart to be an author'. In her diary for 6 February, 1855, some four years earlier, she had noted: 'Lou dreamed that he heard the noise of pens writing'.

The world is full of a number of things,
I am sure we should all be as happy as kings.
A CHILD'S GARDEN OF VERSES

CHAPTER TWO

A Daft-like Laddie

The love of parents for their children is, of all natural affections,
the most ill-starred... Because the parent looks for too much,
or at least something inappropriate, at their offspring's hands,
it is too often insufficiently repaid.
ETHICAL STUDIES

ACCORDING TO THE DUKE OF WELLINGTON, Waterloo was won on the playing fields of Eton. If so, then what battles must have been fought on the playground of Edinburgh Academy? Certainly, the ten-year-old Stevenson found the school in Henderson Row a dangerous place when he was enrolled there in October 1861. After less than four terms in Mr D'Arcy Wentworth-Thomson's class, he retired from the fray, declaring himself a non-combatant scholastically. He would have been happier at home re-enacting the Battle of Waterloo with his army of toy soldiers. He knew every troop movement, having attentively studied this and other famous battles, such as Corunna and Balaclava. Even as a boy, he was something of a military historian, so much so that Henry James always regretted that Stevenson didn't make a career of it in adult life.

His formal education, so tentatively begun at Canonmills and continued in a stutter at Mr Henderson's establishment in nearby India Street, was to be a pattern of fits and starts. The schoolboy Stevenson was a loner. Years in 'the land of counterpane' had taught him to be happy in his own company. Thrown into the world of team games and hearty, boyish comradeship, it was only natural that he should beat a hasty but strategic retreat as soon as he could. At any rate, Tom Stevenson took the view that conventional schooling, or 'teaching boys to sit on their bums', was overrated. Louis was generally apathetic towards school work and possibly for this reason he was never able to spell. Nor did he understand the point of playing a game for the game's sake and he dismissed golf as a mere waste of time. He relented enough to go fishing but was put off by the number of fish he caught – they looked so dead lying beside him on the river bank. In short, Louis impressed neither his schoolmasters nor his classmates. He was only ever to make one enduring school friend, Henry Bellyse Baildon, whom he was to meet in the following year, but not at Edinburgh Academy. Stevenson passed through this distinguished establishment, then only recently founded 'for the education of the sons of gentlemen', without leaving any real mark. His absences were not only due to illness, but also because his parents took him on frequent holidays.

There had been forays to St Andrews, Crieff and Bridge of Allan, but in 1862 he crossed the border into England for the first time. The family stopped in London before crossing the Channel to the real 'abroad' – the Continent. In January 1863 they reached Paris, travelled south to Nice and Menton, and then made their way down the whole spine of Italy, from Genoa to Naples, returning by way of Rome and Florence. Cummy had never been among so many Catholics in her life and her thirteen-year-old charge teased her at every opportunity, telling her, for instance, that the priests behind the curtains hearing confession were really playing cards. His parents were extremely preoccupied with his religious training. Coming at him from three sides as it did, it was a miracle that he didn't turn out a hide-bound Calvinist; but his was a sturdier mentality than they knew. He was comparatively uninspired by the many church and gallery visits. Words were his priority, particularly poetry, and here his mother was his happy, optimistic teacher; they never tired of each other's company.

The party crossed the Brenner Pass (the only time Louis was sick), then on to Vienna and Innsbruck. They sailed up the Rhine to Munich and Nuremberg and Tom Stevenson took the waters in Homburg before returning to London for the train back to Edinburgh. For Louis, this Continental trip was the equivalent of the

Grand Tour of a century earlier. A born traveller, he took it all in his stride. If his conventional education suffered, his unconventional education certainly did not. Besides, whenever they stayed anywhere for longer than a month, a tutor was hired.

In 1863 arrangements were made to transfer him from Edinburgh Academy to (another) Mr Thomson's School 'for backward and delicate boys' in Frederick Street. Louis attracted the attention of street urchins who jeered at him as he walked down to Heriot Row from Mr Thomson's. Cat-calls like 'Hauf a laddie, hauf a lassie, hauf a yella yite' and names like 'daftie' and 'softie' were thrown at him like snowballs, but he refused to acknowledge the insults, rousing his tormentors even further.

The following year it was time for him to face another kind of challenge: boarding-school in England. Mr Wyatt's Burlington Lodge Academy at Spring Grove, Isleworth, Middlesex, was a preparatory school for the larger public schools which were the right of way to Oxbridge, but Louis had no such university ambitions. However, Spring Grove gave him the opportunity to polish his French. It also gave him the chance to co-edit *The Schoolboy's Magazine* with his new friend, Henry Baildon, whose father so disapproved of what he saw before publication – particularly the romantic elements – that he summarily withdrew his son from the project. A life-long correspondent, Baildon's biography of Stevenson appeared in 1901; in 1894 the *Daily News* had published his memoir, 'The Late Mr R.L. Stevenson – A Schoolfellow Remembers', in which he remarks:

In body he was assuredly badly set up. His limbs were long, lean and spidery, and his chest flat, so as almost to suggest some malnutrition, such sharp corners did his joints make under his clothes... The eyes were always genial, however gaily the lights danced in them, but about the mouth there was something a little tricksy and mocking, as if of a spirit that already peeped behind the scenes of life's pageant and more than guessed its realities.

Despite the fact that he had an attack of bleeding from the mouth due to lung congestion, Stevenson actually played football at Burlington Lodge. Apart from that unlikely exertion, nothing had been gained from this English experiment and after only one term he was pleading to come home:

> Dear Papa – You told me to tell you whenever I feel miserable. I do not feel well and I wish to get home.

His father complied. Rather than seeing him as a problem child, his parents seemed to take pleasure in having their son with them much of the time. By the same token, he acquired an early ease in adult company. However, he had to be educated somewhere, despite the fact that he was approaching the age when less privileged Scottish boys were leaving school, rather than trying to find one. The Stevensons' solution was to hire a series of tutors. It was from this time that he began to adopt a certain 'English' air. Anglo-affectations began to creep in and mannerisms develop that were to be so much part of his adult style.

The summer of 1865 was spent with his mother in the Borders town of Peebles where Margaret rented Elibank Villa. There he continued to work with a tutor and composed his first letter in German. He also kept on with his writing – 'I tried to do justice to the inhabitants in the style of *The Book of Snobs.*' He was mostly indoors. He had tried to make friends with the local boys but ended up fighting a mock duel, using real pistols – without bullets in the barrels. To this period belong two works of which no trace remains: *The Baneful Potato*, the libretto for an opera; and 'The Plague-Seller', written at Colinton with his cousin, Henrietta Traquair, of which only a photostat survives, in the collection at Yale University. He also completed the first draft of the play, *Deacon Brodie*, written before going off with his mother to Torquay.

His first taste of publication came to him in 1866 with *The Pentland Rising*. This slight work is really little more than a collection of Covenanting quotations accompanied by juvenile comment, but Tom Stevenson was so pleased with his son's effort that he had it privately printed as a sixteen-page pamphlet by Andrew Elliott in Edinburgh at a cost of three pounds fifteen shillings. A hundred copies were published in November 1866, supposedly to sell at fourpence a copy, but Tom gave them all away to friends. This quaint, spindly little item has accrued considerable valuable today as a literary curiosity.

After Dr Balfour died in 1860, a new minister took over at Colinton and the manse was no longer available for holidays. An alternative retreat was found in Swanston Cottage, at the foot of the Pentland Hills.

> Be it granted me to behold you again in dying
> Hills of home! And to hear again the call;
> Hear about the graves of the martyrs
> The peewees crying
> And hear no more at all.

The locals thought Stevenson a 'daft-like laddie, aye speirin things, an scribblin in his wee books'. Girls were intrigued and there is no doubt that 'this green spot' marked the end of his green years.

In November 1867 he matriculated for Engineering at Edinburgh University. The entry standards were not exacting. In fact, anyone with funds to pay the matriculation and class fees was accepted. Stevenson was in this category. William McLaren remembers him as:

> Fair, tall, a rather narrow figure, a very enquiring mind, and
> very fond of discussing all round anything that interested him,
> or should I say, that did not even peculiarly interest him.

It was not his own decision to put himself forward for a degree in Engineering. Thomas Stevenson was determined that his son should follow in his footsteps. He paid the fees. Victorian fathers were not easy to deter when it came to the matter of their sons' futures.

Louis let himself drift with the tide. It mattered little to him what degree, if any, he took. He wouldn't need it for employment and he didn't want it for any personal satisfaction. He couldn't see himself as a civil engineer: instead of the iron of generations of Stevenson engineers in his blood, he had ink. Nevertheless, there must have been the scent of adventure in his nostrils as he went through the arch at the South Bridge 'at the booming of the hourly bell', smart in his new velvet jacket, ready to step into the 'gaunt quadrangle' and on to another stage of his life.

> All classes rub shoulders on the greasy benches. The raffish young gentleman in gloves must measure his scholarship with the plain, clownish laddie from the parish school.

No one would have taken a bet on Louis getting a degree. He didn't feel he had to attend every lecture, and when he did turn up he sat at the back. Once, asked why he was not taking notes, he replied, 'I'd rather write my own original rubbish.' He would sometimes leave in the middle of a lecture. One contemporary recalled:

> He was always posing, always showing off. The more we jeered, the more he posed – a smile of disdain on his queer, foreign-looking face – so consumed with conceit, he could not even walk without mincing like a dancing master.

His fellow students could not possibly have understood how much this posing was an act of defiant self-defence on Stevenson's part. His behaviour, including the dress idiosyncrasies he affected, was part of a carefully studied re-imaging. His apparent frivolity masked a serious intent to devote his energies to becoming a writer. He would turn his childhood dream of 'the noise of pens writing' into a practical reality. To do so, he only needed time.

> It was not so much that I wished to be an author (though I wished that too) as that I vowed that I would learn to write.

That was a proficiency that tempted me, and I practised to acquire it, as men learn to whittle, in a wager with myself.

Had the same determination been shown in the Engineering course, he would have built a whole string of lighthouses.

All through my boyhood and youth, I was known and pointed out for the pattern of an idler; and yet I was always busy on my own private end, which was to learn to write.

However cavalier his attitude to formal study, he kept his private bargain with himself and worked as hard and as intensely at writing as any other student might do in preparing for a degree exam.

I kept always two books in my pocket, one to read, one to write in. As I walked, my mind was busy fitting what I saw with appropriate words; when I sat by the roadside, I would either read, or a pencil and a penny version-book would be in my hand, to note down the feature of the scene or commemorate some halting stanzas. Thus I lived with words...

And words did not fail him when he applied to the various professors for an attendance certificate, necessary if he were to go on to a second year. The Professor of Greek, John Stuart Blackie, a colourful old Gael who taught his students everything but Greek, could not even remember Stevenson's face when he reported for his certificate. 'Probably not, but I hope that will not prevent you from signing my certificate,' retorted Louis amiably. This caused the old professor to stop humming the Gaelic air on his lips to say '*Quite*', and equally amiably, sign the certificate.

However, the Professor of Engineering was not so lenient. Henry Charles Fleeming Jenkin, a Welshman recently appointed to the Chair, was a formidable polymath. Poet, dramatist and linguist as well as scientist, he saw through Stevenson's sophistry and gave him no chance to try his tricks.

'You have simply not attended my classes, Mr Stevenson.'

There was nothing Stevenson could say to deny that, but, with his belief that, 'What a man truly wants he will get, or he will be changed in the trying' – he tried. Casuistry was already part of his stock in trade. As was charming blandishment. Eventually Jenkin yielded and gave him his certificate, perhaps because he detected the latent worth behind the eighteen-year-old's effrontery, perhaps because he recognised a fellow original, or even perhaps for long-suffering Tom Stevenson's sake. From this unlikely beginning, a great friendship of like minds would later develop. Stevenson remarked, 'I never thought lightly of him afterwards'.

Publicly, Stevenson the Engineering student was quite outrageous in his dilatory attitude. He later recalled himself as a paradoxical figure

> full of changing humours, fine occasional purposes of good, unflinching acceptance of evil... infinite yawnings during lectures and unquestionable gusto in the delights of truancy...

Privately, however, he was the apprentice writer, rigorously bound to a self-imposed regimen of reading, writing and talking, to all of which he applied himself diligently – at home. It was also at home that an incident occurred that was to illustrate this latter aspect of his personality. One afternoon, late in the winter of 1868, Annie Jenkin paid a courtesy call on Margaret Stevenson. They were having tea by the fire when a boy's voice called out from the shadows. Annie Jenkin recalled:

> I listened in perplexity and amazement. Who was this son who talked as Charles Lamb wrote? this young Heine with a Scottish accent? I stayed long and when I came away, the unseen converser came down with me to the front door to let me out. As he opened it, the light of the gas-lamp outside fell on him, and I saw a slender, brown-haired boy, with great dark eyes, a brilliant smile and a gentle, deprecating

bend of the head... looking then, as he always did, younger than his age. I asked him to come and see us. 'Shall I come tomorrow?' he said at once. 'Of course.' I ran home and at dinner I announced to my husband, 'I have made the acquaintance of a poet.'

Annie Jenkin (the first of the three older women Stevenson was to love) might have done anything in the theatre – she could act, sing and play the piano, and was a great beauty. She drew him out of his interior preoccupations and brought him into her world, one in which she and her husband staged their own theatrical productions in their home at 5 Fettes Row. It was time at last for Louis to discard the much-loved toy stage in his bedroom and apply himself to the real thing.

In 'My First Book' he refers to the reams of paper ('now all ash') that had been wasted by this time on ideas for plays. At least he was using these play-writing exercises to 'try and understand the lie of the world'. Like Oscar Wilde and to a lesser extent Kenneth Tynan in a later epoch, Louis saw all of existence as a charade to be played out according to the part – or parts – one was cast to play. He recognised that we grow accustomed to the character we impose upon ourselves; in time, the part becomes the reality. He therefore set out to rehearse the part in which he had cast himself: that of the writer. In this guise he could safely work out all his fantasies on the page.

One role, however, in which he considered himself quite miscast, was that of Lighthouse Engineer. This was borne out when, in the summer of 1868, his father whipped him off on a working holiday along the Fife coast and points north. Intended as part of his practical training in the field, it was to land him instead in the icy waters of the North Sea (in a diving suit), and later, in hot water with his father. He allowed himself to be led from port to port, from Burntisland to Kinghorn, submitting stoically to this 'lighthouse experience'. In Anstruther, 'a grey, grim, sea-beaten hole', he lodged at Cunzie House with Bailie Brown and his wife who insisted on serving him 'chill table beer' with his meals. (He promptly arranged for wine to be sent from Heriot Row.) A bronze plaque now commemorates his stay there, and a carving by Sir Robert Lorimer honours the spot. Stevenson was 'anxious to go slick home... if possible, I should like to cut the business and come right slick out to Swanston'. Instead, it was north to 'sub-Arctic' Wick, via St Andrews and Broughty Ferry. The seas at Wick proved too strong even for Tom Stevenson's skill and experience and he had to admit a rare failure in establishing a harbour wall; but being there gave the seventeen-year-old Stevenson an unforgettable opportunity to go down in a diving suit, before the admiring gaze of the skippers' daughters.

While in Anstruther he attended a performance by strolling players in the town hall in the company of 'young Morrison', an engineering colleague of Stevenson's whose family stayed locally:

A large table placed below the gallery with a print curtain either side of the most limited dimensions was at once the scenery and the proscenium. The manager told us that his scenes were sixteen by twenty-four, and so could not be got in. Though I knew or at least felt sure that there were no such scenes in the poor man's possession, I could not laugh, as the major part of the audience, at this shift to escape criticism.

We saw a wretched farce; and some comic songs were sung. The whole receipt of the evening was 5 and 3d. ... We left soon; and I must say came out as sad as I have been for ever so long; I think the manager had a soul above comic songs. I said this to young Morrison, who is a 'Phillistine' (Matthew Arnold's Philistine, you understand) and he replied, 'how much happier would he be as a common working man'. I told him I thought he would be less happy earning a comfortable living as a shoemaker, than he was starving as an actor, with such artistic work as he had to do. But the Phillistine wouldn't see it. You will observe that I spell Philistine turn about with one and two 'l's.

You will also observe the possessive apostrophe in the letter 'I'. Never mind: the whole epistle shows his complete understanding of the artistic ethos as far as it applies to the performer – which is to suffer gladly in doing the job he loves when he could easily do an ordinary job and enjoy what is laughingly called security. Young Louis is to be applauded for realising this at such a young age. The letter also indicates, however, his congenital difficulty with spelling. It was obviously time to continue his education.

He returned to university, ostensibly to take classes in Latin and Greek but, in reality, to continue his systematic truancy and to experiment further in sartorial eccentricity – with sublime indifference to academic and public opinion. A fellow-student observed:

> His whole appearance was a shock to a puritan neighbourhood. His chestnut hair fell in limp strands over his shoulder. He did not hesitate to dress as a Bohemian; he wore a velveteen jacket like a workman and a grey, flannel shirt to hide his thin arms. And to warm his thin body, he swathed himself like his claimed ancestor, Rob Roy Macgregor, in a dramatic mantle with flowing folds. Some people found him pretentious, others irritating. He was too consciously sensational...

His theatricality could not be denied, nor the fact that he was still the reluctant student:

> I denied myself many opportunities; acting upon an extensive and highly rational form of truantry which cost me a good deal of trouble to put into exercise – perhaps as much as would have taught me Greek.

He refused to study Greek:

> I am sorry indeed that I have no Greek, but I should be sorrier still if I were dead; nor do I know the name of that branch

of knowledge which is worth the acquiring at the price of a brain fever.

By this time, his eccentricity was almost a cult. 'A bundle of affectations... almost suggesting a touch of insanity' commented one disapproving contemporary; another mused retrospectively:

How could we, mere lads, discern the hero and genius in the guise in which he then appeared? We simply saw nothing in him but absurdity because we were stupid. And our failure was the failure of Edinburgh in general. Not till others discovered Robert Louis Stevenson for us did we begin to see what fools we had been. As for the rest of us, it would be no violence to truth to take our present enthusiasm as a measure of our remorse.

There speaks an honest man, and there must have been others because, despite the general derision accorded him in his first session, the highlight of Stevenson's second session was his election to the Speculative Society, in March 1869. ('Oh, I do think the Spec is the best thing in Edinburgh!'). Founded in 1764 as a society for the 'Improvement of Literary Composition and Public Speaking', the Spec was just right for Stevenson the Conservative. One wonders how he got through the process of membership to such a dignified institution. Never mind, he was only too happy to add his name to that of Sir Walter Scott.

About fifty years previously, Scott himself had sailed to the Orkneys, Shetland and the Fair Isles with Stevenson's grandfather, Robert Stevenson, whom he found 'a most gentleman-like and modest man, well-known for his scientific skills'. Now, Stevenson was to repeat the identical journey with his own father in the Northern Lights Commissioners' steamer, the *Pharos*, to make the same inspections his grandfather had made all those years before. It was time to grit his teeth and endure rough seas and unpleasant voyages, but this 'professional' holiday wasn't to prove nearly as bad as he had feared. As Scott had discovered material for *The Pirate*, so Stevenson found the basis for several novels in the storms and seascapes he encountered. He also made a life-long friend in young Edmund Gosse, whom he met on board the *Clansman* as he continued with his father round the Scottish coast to the west and 'over the sea to Skye'. On their trip to the Isle of Earraid he met the artist Sam Bough, who wryly commented: 'You've such a pleasant manner, you know. Quite captivated my wife, you did. She couldn't talk of anything else.'

In the spring of 1871, Stevenson took a train to the Lake District for no other reason, it would seem, than to experience for a few days 'English houses, English faces and English conformation of streets'. But back at university, he was full of doubts about his fitness, in all senses, to be an apprentice engineer. He knew his true vocation to be elsewhere and submitted half-a-dozen contributions to the university magazine, one of which was an essay on 'The Philosophy of Umbrellas'. New heights were reached when his fellow students appointed him editor, and his euphoria lasted as long as the magazine – four editions. The experience only added to his commitment to become a full-time writer. But how could he tell his father?

On 27 March 1871 he read a paper to the Royal Scottish Society of Arts on 'A New Form of Intermittent Light for Lighthouses'. However much the content may have benefited from his father's assistance, it won the Silver Medal and a prize of three pounds for 'a work well worthy of the favourable consideration of the Society, and highly creditable to so young an author'. Tom Stevenson could not have been prouder. It was now that his son decided to put in the dagger. Henrietta Younger, a cousin and childhood playmate was at dinner with the family on that fateful April evening:

> I happened to be in the house when Lou told his father he did not wish to continue to be a civil engineer. This was a terrible blow and disappointment to dear Uncle Tom... [He] was more disappointed still when Lou declared that he wanted to go in for the literary life.

Consternation and uproar. The ladies left the table. The gentlemen guests looked down at their plates. Tight-lipped, Tom told his son that they would discuss the matter further in the morning.

It is as natural and right for a young man to be imprudent ... as it is for old men to turn gray.
CRABBED AGE AND YOUTH

CHAPTER THREE

Love, What is Love?

Youth is wholly experimental
LETTER TO A YOUNG GENTLEMAN

THE WALK FROM HERIOT ROW down Queensferry Road to Cramond Bridge must have seemed a marathon to both men the next morning. After breakfast, his mother had pleaded with Louis to obey his father, and before they set out, she begged her husband to understand their son's point of view. Now she could only wait and see.

Louis had no fear of appearing ludicrous but his Bohemian style must have confounded his father. A fellow student said that he looked as if he were trying to wear out the family trunk of old clothes and wore a tie that looked like 'a strip of old carpet'. Small wonder he was shunned by most respectable folk who did not know him. One lady who saw him in Princes Street remarked on his 'curious way of walking sideways, as if never propelled by any power greater than the wind... floating along like a graceful yacht protecting his sails'. Another Edinburgh resident described him as:

> A slithering, loose, flail of a fellow. All joints, elbows and spindle-shanks, his trousers generally so short in the leg like a scarecrow, that one almost expected him to creak in the wind.

But on that 'dreadful walk', as he was to refer to it, he struck out as sturdily as his father beside him and determinedly stuck to his own point of view – that the world of nuts and bolts and mortar and water was not for him, but that the world of letters was. He would leave university and be a writer, come what may, and though he had nothing to show that he could make a living at it, he assured his father that he would.

Tom Stevenson must have felt that his son was carelessly tossing away his entire heritage. Bear in mind that he had been pressured into his career by his own father, who had been similarly pressured by his father before him, and so on all the way back to Tam Smith. The Balfours had a gentler, but just as professional lineage in the law and the church. There was also the Scottish suspicion of the artist – no kind of artistic vocation could be considered as real work, no matter the talent shown. And what was talent anyway? Could one measure it? Define it? More importantly, could one sell it in the market place? This prejudice added to the enormous weight on Louis to conform. It is to his credit that he fought back so strongly. If tradition was on the father's side, the words were with the son. Just as in his dispute with Fleeming Jenkin, Louis managed to turn his father round and before they turned back at Cramond Brig, they had hit on a compromise. Agreement was reached that Louis would change course for a degree in Law. Tom Stevenson hoped that, as a respectable advocate, his son could keep writing as a sideline. Honour was satisfied. Louis could see that the classical studies involved in a legal course would not be a total waste of time for a man of letters.

Like so many people of genius, Stevenson was essentially an autodidact. However, having battled to give up Engineering, the contest of wills with his father was not quite over. Religious disputes lay ahead. For the moment, they both enjoyed a state of truce and Louis was formally enrolled for lectures in Civil Law, Public Law and the Law of Nature and Nations. (The Chair held for a quarter of a century by his own great-grandfather, James Balfour of Pilrig.)

Louis applied himself to his studies, if not with high enthusiasm, at least a notch or two above the downright apathy of the previous sessions. This new resolve was accompanied by a greater acceptance of the friendship offered by other students, including James Ferrier, Walter Simpson, Robert Glasgow Brown and Charles Baxter. Baxter was to be especially important as the adjutant of all Stevenson's business affairs. In their university days he was a burly Porthos to Stevenson's D'Artagnan, or, perhaps, Soutar Johnny to his Tam o'Shanter. They were a kenspeckle couple, the reed-like Louis and the amply-framed Baxter, two years older and 'with a voice like a column of cavalry'.

Bob Stevenson, who was now studying at the Board of Trustees School of Art, often met up with his cousin for lunch, to which they would depart 'chortling and laughing'. The ebullient Bob was not always a steadying influence. He was the mainspring of the LJR Society founded in jocular spirit in 1872 – LJR stood for Liberty, Justice and Reverence. The Society had a combustible constitution by any standards. 'Liberty' appeared to be nothing more than the freedom to indulge in undergraduate pranks and high jinks. 'Justice' was to be given to new thinking, such as Darwin's Theory of Evolution, which was rocking British Christian society to its very foundations. 'Reverence', having been denied to God, was now given to Art with a capital 'A'.

New occasions teach new duties,
Time makes ancient good uncouth;
They must upward still and onward
Who would keep abreast of truth.

The new rationalism shown by the cousins was perhaps little more than a rush of young blood to the head. Nevertheless, their impious speculations at the Heriot Row table had an explosive effect. Louis was quite unrepentant: 'I, too, have a soul of my own, arrogantly upright, and to that I will listen and conform.' While one feels that this stance was yet more play-acting, it caused even more consternation in Heriot Row than his decision to drop Engineering. Tom Stevenson was an orthodox, if individual, Christian, Margaret a devout daughter of the manse and Cummy a Covenanting fanatic. All three found it impossible to come to terms with his seeming agnosticism.

They don't see either that my game is not the light-hearted scoffer. I believe as much as they do, but generally in the inverse ratio. I am as honest as they and have not come hastily to my views. I reserve, as I told them, many points until I acquire fuller information.

Tom Stevenson was overwhelmed by this turn of events. He did not know where he had gone wrong. As he saw it, he had failed in his God-given patriarchal duties. Louis, on the other hand, had come to see his father's views as a threat to his individual conscience and freedom. He wrote of these 'discussions':

Had I seen the red hell of everything... I should have lied as I have lied so often before... It was rougher than hell, but what can I do?... What the devil am I to do? I own myself an abject idiot.

He did not enjoy hurting or disappointing anyone, not least his parents, but in the winter of 1872 their God was not his God any longer, and this was completely beyond them.

The older and wiser Louis would come to recognise that genuine piety has its own reward, and that the good have no need to be bribed to be holy. As the prayerful patriarch of Vailima, he would say:

To hold the same view at forty as one held at twenty is to have been stupefied for a score of years, and take rank, not as a prophet, but as an unteachable brat.

Reading *Weir of Hermiston*, it is not difficult to see Tom Stevenson in the determined figure of Weir, relentlessly 'climbing the great staircase of his duty' – which brings to mind a speech from Alanna Knight's Stevenson solo play:

It is a particular cross of parents that when a child grows up and becomes himself instead of that pale ideal they had pre-conceived, they must accuse their own harshness or indulgence for this natural result. They have been like the duck and hatched swan's eggs! Or the other way about. Yet they tell themselves, with miserable penitence, that the blame lies with them, and had they sat more closely, the swan would have been a duck, and home-keeping, in spite of it all.

Stevenson found escape in 'performance': his cigarettes could not have raised a more efficient or deliberate smoke-screen than the various zany disguises he adopted throughout his undergraduate years.

On one memorable evening, Bob and Louis got drunk and walked to Fairmilehead after dinner, dancing and singing all the way. 'Such a night is pure gold,' recorded Stevenson. On another occasion he wandered off, this time on his own, and missed dinner at home for the first time in his life. The atmosphere at Heriot Row became so tense that Bob was barred from the door.

Meanwhile, enjoyable and more civilised evenings were spent with the Jenkins, first in Fettes Row, and then at 3 Great Stuart Street, where the couple had their own private theatre. The professor, now free of Louis as an awkward pupil, was happy to receive him as an artistic protégé. They enjoyed sparking off each other. When Louis was still in his Engineering class, the subject of religion had come up, specifically the question of conduct. The professor's ethics were unconventional to say the least. Stevenson had his own excuse: 'I have a genuine morality, but no talent for it.'

'What would Christ have said?' Fleeming had asked.

'Nothing unkind or cowardly,' was the evasive reply.

'True, Mr Stevenson,' came the dry retort, 'nor anything amusing.'

Once Christ's sense of humour had been questioned, His whole divinity, as far as Louis was concerned, was, for a time at least, in doubt. For the moment, however, he would regard the matter, in the practical manner of Scots law, as 'not proven'.

In May 1872 Stevenson was retained as a law clerk at the office of Skene and Peacock, Solicitors and paid a nominal amount to copy letters and familiarise himself with legal practise. While he was in the front office idling over a journal he had just begun, his principal, William Forbes Skene, was in the back room poring over his masterwork, a history of Celtic Scotland, yet the two did not meet.

It must be said that the new law clerk gave his mind less to forensic matters than to his increasing involvement with more congenial things like theatricals. He saw the whole process of play-reading and discussion under 'Madam' Jenkin's direction as 'an oasis in a desert of convention', and in stark contrast to the dining-table tensions at Heriot Row. It was as if in the formidable Jenkin duo he had found another set of parents.

He was too aware of his physical limitations to take himself seriously as an actor, even as an amateur, although he had every instinct for it. He had a good voice, he read well and his natural charm had an immediate effect on any group he joined. He frightened this theatrically-minded set less than he did the unpainted citizenry. More importantly, the involvement cemented his relationship with Fleeming Jenkin. Stevenson unashamedly worshipped the academic. Not that he didn't deserve admiration. Jenkin was engineer enough to have built a toy phonograph ('so that I could teach it to swear'), biologist enough to have corrected Darwin, scientist enough to have written a significant work on fecundity and inventive enough to have pioneered electrical transportation. He was also a first-rate actor in his wife's twice-yearly productions and even wrote a play, *Grizelda*. But what drew Stevenson to him most was his remarkable gift for conversation. Jenkin was the inspiration for Cockshot in 'Talk and Talkers':

> He is possessed by a demoniac energy, welding the elements of
> his life, and bending his ideas as an athlete bends a horseshoe,
> with a visible and lively effort.

He became as much a Stevensonian as Louis was a Jenkinite. At one theatre evening, after Stevenson had read as Aeschylus, Jenkin whispered to the person seated beside him, 'Listen to that boy! He'll be somebody yet.' Stevenson was intermittent in his attendance at rehearsals and performances. Sir J Alfred Ewing (later Principal of Edinburgh University) remembers an occasion when he was on Stage Management and Louis, for once, was in the cast and not, as he usually was, on the Book as Prompter:

> Stevenson was standing in the wings ready to go on in the dress of a Greek Messenger which had been designed by Fleeming with a fidelity that excluded pockets. Louis had omitted to divest himself of a signet ring which he usually wore. Handing it to me he said, 'Wear it till I come off'. We both forgot it that night and next day he vanished into space.

Actually, he went off on his own, to go fishing. An Edinburgh friend who was also on the steamer from Glasgow saw him come off at Dunoon:

> Narrow-chested, bright-eyed, long-haired, wearing on his back a knapsack, which, no doubt, contained a volume of Hazlitt and some bread and cheese.

At Dunoon, an old witch-wife called 'Daft Leezie' read his palm. She prophesied that he would travel much on water and be drowned in it but then she suddenly dropped his hand, and said sadly, 'Black eyes!' She would say no more. Who had 'the old pythoness' seen? Could it have been Fanny Osbourne? Or even Belle Strong? Taking in only the message that he was doomed to drown, he hurriedly rejoined his parents at Bridge of Allan.

During that summer of 1872, he toyed with the idea of going to a German university to study German, but when his mother protested he compromised and went off on holiday with Walter Simpson, son of the famous discoverer of chloroform. They travelled via Brussels to Frankfurt, where they spent every day seeing the sights and every night at the opera. He wrote to his mother from 13 Rosen Gasse:

> An opera is far more real than real life to me. It seems as if

stage illusion and particularly this most hardest to swallow and most conventional illusion of them all – an opera, would never stale upon me. I wish life were an opera. I should like to live in one; but I don't know where I should find a Society so constituted...

One wonders how he managed this Continental jaunt on a law clerk's stipend, even with his father's allowance of half-a-crown a week. However, with the new university session beginning, his pocket money went up to a pound a month, and now he felt he could look for that 'spark of drama in life's drabness' as Jenni Calder puts it, as opposed to the staged reality he had felt in Germany. But then, in a sense, his whole life was a revolving stage, one which revolved around *him*. His view that 'drama is the poetry of conduct and romance the poetry of circumstances' might have been his motto:

Conduct is three parts of life, they say; but I think they put it high. There is a vast deal of life and letters which is not immoral, but simply a-moral; which either does not regard the human will at all, or deals with it in obvious and healthy relations; where the interest turns, not upon what the man shall choose to do, but on how he manages to do it...

Incidentally, following the Royal Society's positive reception of his paper on 'Intermittent Light for Lighthouses' Louis addressed the Society on the subject of 'The Thermal Influence of Forests' in May 1873. It was all in the realm of performance. So was his address to the Speculative Society around the same time, when he explained, no doubt through a barrage of ribaldry, that he was, among other things, the cleverest person of his age 'between here and California'. This assertion did not prevent his being elected President of the Society. He could not have been aware of the prophetic overtones – the presumptuous student would see California much sooner than he expected, in the role of amateur emigrant.

Busy with his extramural activities, Stevenson otherwise gained his university education by osmosis. However, he sometimes displayed his genuine authority in literary matters. For instance, at one tutorial his grasp of Scott astonished Reverend Bisset, his philosophy lecturer. For all he professed that he had little Latin, he took to Virgil under the scholarly William Sellar. He gained his only certificate of merit from Professor Kelland, the Professor of Mathematics. Mostly he kept to himself the extraordinary range of his private reading before and during his student years:

> Shakespeare has served me best. Few living friends have had upon me an influence so strong for good as Hamlet or Rosalind. The last character, already well beloved in the reading, I had the good fortune to see, I must think, in an impressionable hour, played by Mrs Scott Siddons. Nothing has ever more moved, more delighted, more refreshed me; nor the influence quite passed away. Kent's brief speech over the dying Lear had a great effect upon my mind, and was the burthen of my reflections for long; so profoundly, so touchingly generous did it appear in sense, so overpowering in expression.

He had virtually lived with Shakespeare since the nursery, having it read to him by his mother before he could read himself, and now he found Dumas and Meredith (who in later years was to become a friend) and soaked up the best he could find in virtually every field of writing. He knew that if any good work was to be done, a study of the masters was called for. Starting early with Shakespeare and the Bible, he gradually read his way through his childhood and down the whole mountain of literature.

> I have played the sedulous ape to Hazlitt, to Lamb, to Wordsworth, to Sir Thomas Browne, to Defoe, to Montaigne, to Baudelaire and to Oberman...

The last-named does not immediately spring to mind as one of the great masters, but Louis would have learned something from him. Such was his enthusiasm for the printed word, he would have got something from anything in print. Yet he was becoming increasingly aware that there were things in life other than pens and paper. There was so much he still had to experience. Like falling in love, for instance.

There may have been sexual skirmishes in North Berwick and Dunblane and more serious entanglements in Swanston. There was also James Ferrier's sister, 'Coggie', whom he admired, and Walter Simpson's sister, Eve, who, unfortunately, did not admire him. No matter these casual occasions, he had never fully declared himself as far as any woman was concerned. Perhaps 'de-Claire' is the better spelling. The enigma of 'Claire', the girl he was supposed to have loved in his wilder student days, still persists in Stevenson lore despite being debunked by Stevenson authorities such as Furnas and Mehew. Myth, however, is a determined weed, and difficult to eradicate totally. 'Claire' is held by some biographers to have been the prostitute Kate Drummond, a well-born Highland girl who was thrown on to the streets by an outraged father; or 'Mary H', the prostitute whom Stevenson said he knew in the 'way of her business'.

Perhaps as another ploy in his 'shocking' game, he disconcerted his parents with threats to bring a lady of the night home as his bride. They were increasingly anxious about his moral wellbeing and it was speedily arranged that he visit his mother's relatives in Suffolk and in the summer of 1873 his father saw him onto a southbound train. If Louis did not go altogether happily, any journey held potential for adventure. He was always ready to start on the next phase – but who would he be this time? Which Louis would he present, or had he run his full gamut of personalities already? He had plenty of time on the train to ponder. He enjoyed looking out of the window of a railway carriage at life rushing by...

Faster than fairies, faster than witches,
Bridges and houses, hedges and ditches;
And charging along like troops in a battle,

All through the meadows the horses and cattle:
All of the sights of the hill and the plain
Fly as thick as driving rain;
And ever again, in the wink of an eye,
Painted stations whistle by...

He was gathering speed himself, and heading into further complications. Cockfield Rectory in Sudbury, Suffolk was the home of one of his Balfour cousins, Maude, and her husband the Reverend Churchill Babington. He had stayed with them before, but this time he arrived, hot and dusty and unannounced, although expected. Another house guest, Fanny Sitwell, witnessed his arrival:

That afternoon I was lying on a sofa near an open window when I saw a slim youth in a black velvet jacket and straw hat, with a knapsack on his back, walking up the avenue. 'Here is your cousin,' I said to Mrs Babington, and she went to meet him... Then the hours began to fly by as they had never flown before in that dear, quiet old Rectory... his talk was like nothing I had ever heard before, though I knew some of our best talkers and writers. Before three days were over, I wrote to Sidney Colvin... and begged him (with Mrs Babbington's leave) not to delay his promised visit if he wanted to meet a brilliant, and to my mind, unmistakable young genius called Robert Louis Stevenson...

If he impressed *her*, she absolutely stunned *him*. Frances Jane Featherstonehaugh Sitwell was married to an alcoholic Irish clergyman and had a son. The Irishwoman became his Muse, his Consuelo, his Madonna and his first adult sexual passion. Estranged from her husband, she had an 'understanding' with Sidney Colvin, a Cambridge professor, and she did not encourage Louis. In fact, she dealt with him so gently and with such tact and grace that he felt his infatuation all the more. The Stevenson performance in Suffolk was that of the *chevalier servant* in the long tradition of the chivalrous knight with the ideal of a chaste love made manifest in his lady. The arrival of the bespectacled professor helped resolve the delicate situation.

> Love, what is love?
> A great and aching heart,
> Wrung hands and silence,
> And a great despair...

The coincidence here was that just as Fanny Sitwell replicated Annie Jenkin, Colvin slid nicely into Fleeming Jenkin's role as mentor for Louis. Indeed, he was to be a lifelong influence and a very close friend indeed. But that was in the future. For the present, Louis desolately accepted the hopelessness of his feelings and 'tried to read a little Law'. On Colvin's suggestion during their walks around the rectory grounds, he tried his hand at some magazine articles. Both Colvin and Fanny realised that if the young man could write as well as he talked, he was publishable.

With Colvin's encouragement, he worked out a short story, 'Roads', which he sent to the London *Saturday Revue*. It was promptly rejected. Brought back to earth by this assessment of his first attempt at writing professionally, he returned to Edinburgh. He had only intended to stay a week at the rectory but had stayed a month.

He could not forget Fanny Sitwell:

> If I had wings, my lady, like a dove,
> And knew the secrets of the air,
> I should be gone, my lady, to my love
> To kiss the sweet division of your hair,
> If I had wings, my lady, like a dove.
> For all is sweet, my lady, in my love,
> Sweet hair, sweet breast and sweeter eyes
> That draw my soul, my lady, like a dove,
> Drawn southward by the shining of the skies,
> For all is sweet, my lady, in my love.

If I could die, my lady, with my love,
Die, mouth to mouth, a splendid death,
I should take wing, my lady, like a dove,
To spend upon her lips, my all of breath,
If I could die, my lady, with my love.

And he wrote to her:

if I never saw you again, and lived all my days in Arabia, I
should be reminded of you continually. You have gone all
over the house of my mind and left everywhere sweet traces
of your presence.

Even so, at her request, he eventually burned every letter she
had ever sent to him at Heriot Row, letters which continued spo-
radically, until he left for America in 1879. She, it must be noted,
kept every word that Louis wrote to her, although she refused to
make them available for publication in her lifetime, regarding them
as 'too sacred to print'. Their relationship was a vital part of his
growing-up. As it happened, Fanny Sitwell and Sidney Colvin did
not marry until 1903, after his mother and her husband were dead,
by which time Colvin was fifty-six, she sixty-two – and Stevenson
had been dead for seven years.

In the autumn of 1873, Louis accompanied his father to Leven in
Fife and then with both parents went to Glasgow where he and his
mother shopped while Tom attended to business. The trio continued
on to Helensburgh and Dumfries, where the sight of Burns's house
made Louis 'deeply sad'. Feeling altogether down, he returned with
his parents to their favourite Dunblane, where he took to solitary
walks in the woods and wrote to Baxter:

When I am a very old and respectable citizen with white hair
and bland manners and a gold watch, I shall hear three crows
cawing in my heart, as I heard them this morning. I vote for
old age and eighty years of retrospect.

He may have shrugged off the Dunoon gypsy's warning, yet he had his own premonition; in the same letter, he continued, 'yet, after all, I dare say, a short shrift and a nice green grave are about as desirable'.

By this time his passion for Fanny Sitwell had more or less spent itself but they remained good friends and he tried to see her whenever he was in London, usually at Colvin's house in South Norwood. On one such visit late in 1873 he fell seriously ill and on medical advice was dispatched at once to the Riviera. At least he was back in his beloved France. That December, 'Roads' appeared in *Portfolio* magazine, possibly as a result of Colvin's influence. This marked Stevenson's debut as a professional writer, for he received a cheque for three pounds eight shillings on its publication. He had attained his life's ambition to become a paid author. He signed this inaugural essay 'L.S. Stoneven'.

As soon as he was well again he returned to Edinburgh to give some attention to his Law degree. Though he never meant to practise, he had at least to qualify. Besides, his father had promised him a thousand pounds on graduation. Nobody is quite sure what Stevenson got up to in the winter of 1873. Although ostensibly given to a study of Commercial and Political Economy, Scots Law and Medical Jurisprudence, the trail becomes rather murky and we lose him among the wynds and closes of Edinburgh's Old Town:

Looking back on it, I am surprised at the courage with which I first ventured alone into the societies in which I moved; I was the companion of seamen, chimney-sweeps and thieves; my circle was being continually challenged by the action of the Police Magistrate. I see now the little sanded kitchen where 'Velvet Coat' (for such was the name I went by) has spent days together, generally in silence and making sonnets in a penny-version book; and, rough as the material may appear, I do not believe these days were among the least happy I have spent. I was distinctly petted and respected: the women were most gentle and kind with me...

He had always sought the alternative, probably as a rough revenge for being born a weakling, but 'what's bred in the bone will out in the flesh', and the flesh was indeed weak. He now assumed an ostentatious grubbiness, offending not only his household, but friends and neighbours, some of whom cut him dead in the street. He seemed determined to follow Robert Fergusson, whom he admired as 'a wild boy. Of such a mixed strain, so unfortunate, and, as I always felt, so like myself'. The brilliant eighteenth century poet had spiralled into dereliction and died at only twenty-three – the very age Stevenson now was.

Stevenson did not seem to care if he was ostracised by respectable Edinburgh society. He was reciprocally affronted by their hypocrisy:

> O fine, religious, decent folk
> In Virtue's flaunting gold and scarlet,
> I sneer between two puffs of smoke,
> Give me the publican and harlot.

He had deliberately turned his back on the New Town to claim the Old. He would sometimes stand on the North Bridge and enviously watch the southbound trains, then stroll through the Grassmarket and the Cowgate drinking it all in:

> I love night in the city
> The lighted streets and the swinging gait of harlots
> I love cool, pale morning
> In the empty bye-streets,
> With only here and there a female figure,
> A slavey with lifted dress and a key in her hand,
> A girl or two at play in the corner of waste-land
> Tumbling and showing their legs and crying out to me
> loosely.

He was the bending beatnik, with notebook at the ready, on the trail of happenings and experience to store as fodder against his future writing days.

*For God's sake, give me a young
man who has brains enough
to make a fool of himself.*
CRABBED AGE AND YOUTH

CHAPTER FOUR

The Reluctant Advocate

*All my old opinions were only stages on the
way to the one I now hold, as it itself is
only a stage on the way to something else.*
CRABBED AGE AND YOUTH

THE 'ENGLISHING' OF RLS continued with his meeting with Colvin
and his introduction to the Savile Club in Mayfair. These two fac-
tors combined to form the beginnings of Stevenson's London circle.
Colvin had visited him in Menton early in 1874 and probably took
back another essay, 'Ordered South', which appeared in *Macmillan's
Magazine* that May. Stevenson received five pounds, a couple more
than for his previous piece. Meanwhile *Portfolio* had taken another
two articles. He was on his way as an author, but there was still the
matter of his Law degree.

With some reluctance, he returned to London and made a
tentative approach to the English Bar, without great hope. After
a discouraging medical consultation with Sir Andrew Clark in
Cavendish Square, he resigned himself to returning to Edinburgh
and opening his Scottish law books again. Then, quite suddenly, he
was in London again. Almost fortuitously, he collapsed in Colvin's
house in Hampstead. Immediate rest and warmth was advised and
that, for Louis, meant the South of France. During another extended
stay at Menton he visited the casino at Monte Carlo with Colvin
and met Andrew Lang, who was on holiday in the Riviera. Lang
was not impressed – 'Girlish-looking', he recorded. Yet eventually
Lang became a friend, 'dear Andrew, with the brindled hair'.
Nevertheless, he would remain uncomfortable at his friend's
eccentric appearance: meeting him by chance in Bond Street, he

once exclaimed, 'No, no, Louis, go away! My character will stand a great deal, but it won't stand being seen with a "thing" like you in Bond Street'. By the time of this encounter, Stevenson had stopped wearing the magnificent cloak Colvin had bought for him in Paris. Knowing his young friend's taste for the conspicuous, instead of buying the plain overcoat requested, Colvin had purchased a cloak, 'piratical in appearance, in the style of the 1830s, dark blue and flowing, and fastening with a snake-buckle'. Stevenson was thrilled, and wrote to his father:

> My cloak is the most admirable of all garments. For warmth, unequalled; for a sort of pensive, Roman stateliness, some-times warming into Romantic guitarism, it is without con-current; it stands alone. If you could see me in my cloak it would impress you... It is a fine thought for absent parents that their son possesses the GREATEST vestment in Menton.

His candid pleasure in dress disarms any criticism of him as a *poseur*. He was never to lose his delight in the sartorial. It extended to his brief flurry with stage costume – his finery as the Duke in *Twelfth Night* quite enthralled him, even if the part didn't.

With winter over, it was again time to return home. He made a snail's progress of it, stopping over in Paris to see Bob at his studio in Boulevard St-Michel. This was the first time Louis had been in Paris without his parents, and he took good advantage of it. He and Bob spent two weeks thoroughly investigating the Latin Quarter in the company of the American artist, Will Low, then all three visited the artists' colony at Barbizon. Louis enjoyed an idyllic stay at Siron's Inn, taking solitary walks through the Forest of Fontainebleau. He managed to get some words down on Victor Hugo before getting back to London, a confirmed Francophile. He spent a further two weeks with Colvin, during which time he saw Fanny Sitwell. Finally back in Edinburgh, he felt not only better in health, but also better for the fact that he 'had made a real start in the profession which had so long been his ambition'. He was well aware of the gravity of abandoning Engineering.

Say not of me that weakly I declined
The labours of my sires, and fled the sea
The towers we founded, and the lamps we lit
To play at home with paper like a child.

On his arrival home, his father was so pleased to see him that he upped his allowance to eighty-four pounds per annum – which, 'for dignity's sake', Stevenson preferred to consider in French francs, because it sounded more. One part of him would have liked to be independent from his father, the other knew when he was well off.

The Law degree still hung over him. He hurried off to Swanston to read up on Roman Law, but instead, caught a cold. Despite feeling miserable, he finished the article on Victor Hugo and sent it off to Leslie Stephen's *Cornhill*. To his surprise, he received not only a cheque but a friendly, four-page critique that would have been invaluable to any young author. This article was his first published work to bear the famous initials 'RLS'.

John Morley of *The Fortnightly* now asked him to review Lord Lytton's *Fables in Song* – which he duly did. He was leading 'a funny life', working and studying, going for walks in the hills around Swanston and in the evening, 'having a couple of pipes' with his father. It was an old man's life for someone who was just twenty-three, 'yet it is surprising how it suits me, and how happy I keep'.

On 3 June 1874 he was back in London to be formally elected to membership of the Savile Club, his proposers being Sidney Colvin and Fleeming Jenkin. Among the sponsors was Andrew Lang. Tom Stevenson was only too pleased to pay the required fee of ten guineas – 'as an advance'. The Club, founded in 1868 in Savile Row, was now in Brook Street premises 'tastefully decorated with playbills and umbrella... the hats of many rising authors depended at regular intervals along the walls.' He was an eminently clubbable man, as Colvin put it, 'habitually surrounded as a radiatory centre of good talk, a kind of ideal incarnation of the spirit of the Society'.

> Here gather daily those young eaglets of glory, the swordsmen of the pen, who are the pride and wonder of the world... They are all young, and youth is a great gift. They are all clever authors... And they are all Rising.

However, despite Leslie Stephen's efforts to introduce him to Thomas Carlyle in Chelsea, Carlyle refused to see him. Quite unperturbed, Stevenson returned to Edinburgh. The Sage of Ecclefechan was not missed by young Mr Stevenson.

He got back to find that his cousin Bob was seriously ill with diphtheria. He recovered, but Louis was shaken. He and Bob were more like brothers than cousins and he was more than happy to act as David Copperfield to Bob's Steerforth. Bob always took the initiative. In 'Talk and Talkers', Stevenson portrayed him as Spring-Heel'd Jack:

> In the Spanish proverb, the fourth man necessary to compound a salad is a mad man to mix it; Jack is that madman... He doubles like a serpent, changes and flashes like a changing kaleidoscope, transmigrates bodily into the views of others, and so, in the twinkling of an eye and with a heady rapture, turns questions inside out and flings them empty before you on the ground like a triumphant conjurer.

Louis now went on a yachting cruise in the Hebrides with Walter Simpson. It was a busy summer. He wrote 'John Knox and his Relations with Women' and 'An Appeal to the Clergy of the Church of Scotland'. In August, he went on holiday with his parents to Chester and then to Llandudno in Wales. He had the idea of going to Poland to visit a friend, but instead went walking in the Chilterns. His train back to Edinburgh in November was delayed for three hours by severe weather and he came into Waverley Station to find his father standing on the platform looking like a snowman.

The strain of all this activity told, and he saw in the New Year of 1875 'crying and shaking badly', unable to work for more than an hour a day. This didn't prevent him for long from taking part in concerts and plays, splendidly attired in his pirate's cloak. Charlotte McDonald was in the audience at a performance of Wagner's *Flying Dutchman* and later noted that he had talked to his neighbour throughout, 'His rather unusual appearance... made him conspicuous and affected-looking among the crowd.' He revealed another side to Fanny Sitwell, in a letter of February 1875:

> O, I have such a longing for children of my own; yet do not think I could bear it if I had one. I fancy I must feel more like a woman than like a man about that. I sometimes hate the children I see in the street – you know what I mean by hate – wish they were somewhere else, and not there to mock me; and sometimes, again, I don't know how to go by them for love of them, especially the very wee ones.

Whatever its sentimentality, this shows a touching, unexpected aspect of the Stevenson too often obscured by his own self-generated obfuscations. In the same letter, continued on the Saturday of that same week, he went on in another vein:

> Yesterday, Leslie Stephen, who was down here to lecture, called on me and took me up to see a poor fellow, a sort of poet who writes for him and who has been eighteen months in our infirmary, and may be, for all I know, eighteen months more. It was very sad to see him there, in the little room with two beds, and a couple of sick children in the other bed; a girl came in to visit them and they played dominoes on the counterpane... The gas flared and crackled, the fire burned in a dull, economical way; Stephen and I sat in a couple of chairs and the poor fellow sat up in his bed with his hair and

beard all tangled, and talked as cheerfully as if he'd been in a king's palace, or the great King's palace of the blue air. He has taught himself two languages since he has been lying there. I shall try to be of use to him..

William Ernest Henley, thus brought into his life as an object of charity, was to become one of the greatest friends he would ever know. In the strange theatre-land that Stevenson had made of his own existence, the action suddenly changed scene, to what can only be called 'another part of the forest'. It is impossible to overestimate Henley's importance in his development as a man and as an artist. He had somehow made his way by boat to Edinburgh from Gloucester in 1873, penniless and not knowing a soul in Scotland, to ask the eminent surgeon Joseph Lister to save his good leg from tuberculosis. The disease had already cost him the other. Lister, impressed by the young Englishman's grit and intelligence, agreed to take him on as a non-paying patient. He was given a room at the Royal Infirmary, which Henley later described in a poem as 'corridors of stone and iron, cold, naked, clean, half-workhouse and half-jail'.

Henley had to submit daily to the excruciating scraping of his half-leg, but otherwise had to lie all day in bed. Leslie Stephen had hoped Stevenson might 'bring him some books, or even read to him... and be otherwise useful' Before long he was visiting regularly. One day he carried an armchair on the top of his head from Heriot Row to the Infirmary, all the way up the Mound and along George IV Bridge. If he was going to do charitable work, he was going to do it comfortably.

Henley and Stevenson were both outsiders, by virtue of their respective physical handicaps forced to be spectators, although they yearned to be activists. They had the stuff of heroes in them, but no outlet other than words.

On their occasional excursions, Stevenson would push Henley in a wheelchair through the Old Town, much like Osric pushing Falstaff through Cheapside. They shared a great love and knowledge of Shakespeare and a passion for theatre. If Stevenson could talk at length about Madam Jenkin, Henley could counter with having seen Henry Irving and Ellen Terry; and he also remembered Dickens's 'long, white finger and a flashing jewel', as he performed his famous Readings. Henley was only a year older than Stevenson but he seemed to have lived in another world and in another time. In his essay on Dumas, also a Stevenson favourite, Henley described the Frenchman as 'a prodigy of force and industry, a great artist in many varieties of form, a prince of talkers and storytellers, one of the kings of the stage…' He could have been describing himself. Stevenson quickly came under his spell. Their meetings were fuelled by debate, discussion and disagreement. Like Fleeming Jenkin, Henley was a polymath, like Stevenson, an autodidact, and like Colvin, a critic. Given that life had dealt him such a poor hand, he was surprisingly confident and wholly original. After all that he had come through, Fate held no terrors for William Henley. He sounded his own trumpet-blast, defiantly, not only to the world of letters, but to the world at large:

> It matters not how strait the gait,
> How charged with punishments, the scroll,
> I am the master of my fate,
> I am the captain of my soul.

Those are his own words, and none could be more indicative of the man. During the summer, the family phaeton went between Swanston and Edinburgh twice a day. When Stevenson borrowed it to take Henley to the countryside, merely getting him to the carriage was a challenge in itself:

> I had a business to carry him down the long stair, and more of a business to get him up again, but while he was in the carriage it was splendid. It is now just the top of spring with us. The whole country is mad with green. To see the cherry-blossom bitten out upon the black firs and the black firs bitten out of the blue sky was a sight to set before a king…

Again the royal allusion. Stevenson's reward for such generous activity was summed up in his own comment – 'The look on his face was wine to me.' If Stevenson had allowed his new friend to breathe in the scents of the countryside again, then the boisterous Henley must also have been a breath of fresh air to Stevenson. Their tirade of talk, by the bedside or on their 'excursions', must have touched on all things. Stevenson would undoubtedly have heard all about Henley's drab childhood, his clever, if unbalanced, brothers, and of how the tuberculosis had robbed him of a place at Oxford. Henley would have heard about Tom Stevenson, Bob Stevenson, Fleeming Jenkin and Sidney Colvin. He would also have learned of the female presences in Stevenson's life – Cummy, his mother, his Aunt Jane, Madam Jenkin and Mrs Sitwell – especially Mrs Sitwell. Henley would have expressed a robust opinion of that delicate situation. He would have recommended direct action wherever sex was involved, preferably not with surrogate mothers. No doubt Henley would have wanted to know more about 'Claire' – in whatever guise Stevenson chose to portray her.

Henley might have been surprised by his friend's attitude to prostitutes – 'What man would have their courage?' – and with women generally, seen by Stevenson as victims 'of man and nature', who were forced to cope with the 'tedious and infantile vanity of the other sex'. He also surmised that there would be no children if men had to bear them. The Henley approach was more Burnsian than Stevensonian.

In 'Talk and Talkers', the character of 'Burly' is based on Henley:

There is something boisterous and piratic in Burly's manner of talk... he will roar you down, he will bury his face in his hands, he will undergo passions of revolt and agony; and meanwhile, his attitude of mind is both conciliatory and receptive... Throughout there has been the perfect sincerity, perfect intelligence, and a desire to hear, although not always to listen...

Stevenson's birthplace, Howard Place, Edinburgh.
A painting by Robert Hope.

Alison Cunningham – from a painting by J Fiddes Watt, 1908.

Margaret Stevenson with Louis, 1854.

No. 17 Heriot Row 'with a lamp before the door', 1857.
From a painting by Robert Hope.

Thomas Stevenson with Louis. Father and son *c.* 1857.

The Stevenson family with maids outside a holiday home, *c.* 1865.

Swanston Cottage, the Stevensons' summer house from 1867.
A painting by Robert Hope.

Skelt's cut-out figures.

The Davos Press, a toy for Lloyd, a tool for RLS, *c.* 1882.

Lloyd, Fanny and RLS at Saranac Lake with servant and big dog, *c.* 1888.

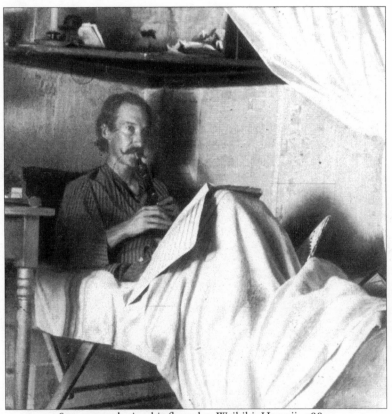

Stevenson playing his flageolet, Waikiki, Hawaii, 1889.

The *Equator* at wharf in Honolulu, 1889.

On the deck of the *Equator*.

Louis and Lloyd with friends at the San Souci bar, Butaritari Island.

The tattooed legs of Vaitepu, Queen of the Marquesas Islands.

A portrait of RLS in Sydney sent to Charles Baxter in 1893.

Henley responded with 'The Apparition':

Thin-legged, thin-chested, slight unspeakably
Neat-footed, and weak-fingered: in his face –
Lean, dark-boned, curved of beak and touched with race,
Bold-lipped, rich-tinted, mutable as the sea,
The brown eyes radiant with vivacity –
There shines a brilliant and romantic grace,
A spirit intense and rare, with subtle trace
Of feminine force and energy.
Valiant in velvet, light in ragged luck,
Most vain, most generous, sternly critical,
Buffoon and lover, poet and sensualist:
A deal of Ariel, just a streak of Puck,
More Cleopatra, of Hamlet most of all,
And something of the shorter catechist.

To assuage family sensitivities, Henley replaced 'Of feminine force' with 'Of passion, impudence', and dropped 'More Cleopatra' in favour of 'Much Antony'. He encapsulates the spirit of RLS in what is virtually a declaration of love – the two men did love each other, in the platonic sense. Henley's poem takes its place, with Sargent's portrait and Neri's painting of the older Stevenson, as one of the true likenesses of the real RLS.

When Henley had to return to the Infirmary for the final phase of his treatment Stevenson was thrown back on his own resources. He could never resist an opportunity to escape from Edinburgh, this time to visit Bob in Paris. The pair enjoyed a short trip to Barbizon before Stevenson returned to Edinburgh for rehearsals of *Twelfth Night* with the Jenkin troupe. That April he wrote to Fanny Sitwell:

I have thrown off the worst of my depression; indeed this morning I can scarcely call myself depressed. I am a little 'February' that's all. I am to play Orsino in *Twelfth Night* at the Jenkins. I could not resist that; it is such a delightful part... I rehearsed yesterday from quarter-to-seven and today from four (with interval for dinner) till eleven. I play Orsino every day in all the pomp of Solomon, splendid Francis the First clothes, heavy with gold and stage jewellery. I play it ill enough, I believe; but me and the clothes, and the wedding wherewith me and the clothes are reconciled, produce every night a thrill of admiration. Our cook told my mother (There is a servants' night, you know) that she and the housemaids were 'juist prood tae be able tae say it was oor young gentlemen'.

Despite the approval from below stairs, everyone, not least Stevenson himself, was aware that he kept his best acting for his off-stage performances.

It was around this time that he met William Seed from New Zealand. Seed fired his imagination with his talk of the South Seas. The strands of Stevenson's life were beginning to come together, although the pattern of the final design wasn't quite clear as yet.

Nothing of his experience was to be wasted, and there were some new ones: he went canoeing on the Firth of Forth and made his first acquaintance with the Hawes Inn at South Queensferry.

He took to wearing his boating flannels with a straw hat, or a silver pork pie hat with his pirate's cloak: anything to outrage the decorous conventions of Princes Street. Henley, having been released from hospital, now lived in a garret high above the same street. He described Stevenson dressed up for a social evening:

in a dress coat, a blue flannel shirt, pepper and salt trousers, silk socks and patent leather shoes. He was exceedingly vain of foot – which were neat and elegant. His hair fell to his collar; he waltzed, he talked, he exploded, he was altogether wonderful. And the women, (this would have touched him had he known it) were in fits of laughter till – the whole Romantic Movement in his cloak and turban – he departed

to dream (it may be) of a sentence of Sir Thomas Browne's
and a gin and ginger at Rutherford's.

As we have seen, his sartorial extravagance was an expression
of his rebelliousness. But the Edinburgh he so scandalised would
not have recognised him in daytime mode, sweating over the anvil
of his creativity, beating out his prose into saleable articles.
However, there was just as much thrown out as sent out, and he
would always remain the hardest critic of his own work.

Oh, when shall I find the story of my dreams, that shall never
halt nor wander nor step aside, but go ever before its face, and
ever swifter and louder, until the pit receives its roaring.

The writer in him is evident in every line of this Blake-like prose.
But, for the moment, it was the Writer to the Signet that beckoned.
The fateful day was upon him – 14 July, his final Bar Examination.
The formal part of his degree was a six-page thesis on Justinian's
Pandects (Book 41, Title 9). His subject was the distinction between
Pro Dote and *Pro Suo* as these apply to a person's state before and
after marriage. His submission deserves to be recognised as one
of his better pieces of acting, for his performance at the *viva voce*
far outstripped anything he ever did for Madam Jenkin. Professor
Macpherson had asked him to define marriage, and Stevenson an-
swered with the definition straight out of Erskine:
   'Marriage is the conjunction of man and woman in the strictest
society of life till death shall separate them.'
   'And what is demurrage?
   'A delay in resolution. A waiting period.'
   'Just so, Mr Stevenson...'
The answers were delivered in so pat a fashion as to suggest
comprehensive home study (which we know was not the case), a
fluke of preparation (which is a possibility) – or that he had a fair
idea of what would be asked. This has been hinted at by some Stevensonian authorities, based on a rumour that some students had

stumbled on the set question. Whatever the case, he got through the *viva voce*, and that was all that was required. The Professor of French was amazed at Stevenson's fluency. 'You speak it like a Frenchman,' he said. But when he expressed concern about his grammatical lapses, Stevenson was quick to explain that these were because he spoke like a Frenchman. Shades of Fleeming Jenkin. With yet another examiner, he avoided answering questions on a book he had not read by expounding fulsomely on its lack of literary merit. Stevenson effectively talked himself into a degree in Law. He was duly passed for the Scottish Bar, having been 'found qualified and recommended'. At the end of the day, he came out of the examination room in the company of the examining professors 'all of them looking very jolly'. Jenkin sent him an encouraging note:

Accept my heartiest congratulations on being done with it. I believe that is the view you like to take of the beginning you have just made.

For the sake of appearances, a brass plate was set up outside Heriot Row, announcing 'R.L. Stevenson, Advocate'. A wig and gown were bought, a new dress suit ordered, but it was all a gesture. He walked up and down Parliament House a few times, feeling ill-at-ease in his lawyers robes, the butt of ridicule from his fellow barristers. He did make a few appearances in court, relying on solicitors and friendly judges to see him through. His total earnings from the Scottish Bar that winter amounted to four guineas from four briefs. What was worse, his father deferred the promised thousand pounds due on his graduation 'until he had matured'. Stevenson took his revenge by annihilating his father nightly at the dinner table. Young Flora Masson was present on one such occasion:

Our end of the table was, to me, uncomfortably brilliant. Mr Stevenson had taken me in and Louis Stevenson was on my other side. Father and son both talked, taking diametrically opposite points of view on all things under the sun... [Louis] was on that evening in one of his most recklessly brilliant moods. His talk was almost incessant. I remember feeling quite dazed at the amount of intellect he expanded on each subject, however trivial in itself, that we touched upon. He worried it, as a dog might worry a rat, and threw it off lightly, as some chance word set him thinking, and talking, of something else.

The father's face at certain moments was a study – an indescribable mixture of vexation, fatherly pride and admiration, and sheer bewilderment at the boy's brilliant flippancies, and the quick, young thrust of his wit and criticism. Our talk turned on realism and the duty of the novelist... father and son debated with some heat the subject of word coinage and the use of modern slang. Mr Stevenson upheld the orthodox doctrine of a 'Well of English Undefiled' which of course made Louis rattle off with extraordinary ingenuity whole sentences composed of words of foreign origin taken into our language from all over the world... [and] proved the absurdity of such a doctrine and indeed its practical impossibility. It was a real feat in the handling of language, and I can see to this day his look of pale triumph.

Was this the boy who was said to have no general scholarship?

Lack of funds prevented any further escapes to London, so he celebrated the New Year of 1876 by taking the train to Ayr and walking to Maybole, Girvan, Ballantrae, Stranraer, Glenluce and Wigtown then turning it into 'A Winter's Walk in Carrick and Galloway' which he sold to the *Illustrated London News*. He returned to Edinburgh refreshed enough to read the part of Richard the Second twice at the Shakespeare Union at the end of February. For this he wore an embroidered smoking cap and a velvet jacket and was swathed in his famous blue pirate's cloak.

I have been studying how I may compare
This prison where I live unto the world.

And, for because the world is populous
And here is not a creature but myself,
I cannot do it. Yet I'll hammer it out...

That he did so was borne out by JM Harkom of the Edinburgh Shakespeare Society:

What helped to impress the two evenings in the memory was the remarkable likeness of the future novelist to the ancient fresco portrait of Richard the Second in Westminster Abbey... his whole expression while reading the play was remarkably suggestive of the original.

Thus the educational phase of his life ends, with him on the stage, all dressed up but with nowhere to go.

Hey diddle-diddle, the cat and the fiddle,
The cow jumped over the moon,
From circumference to middle,
The whole is a riddle,
And I hope to be out of it soon.

The ex-engineer, now an ex-barrister, was at last free to express himself in his own way. He hadn't quite wiped off all the greasepaint however. Seeing the great Italian actor Tommaso Salvini as Macbeth at the Theatre Royal, he had the nerve to write a review of the performance and send it to the *Academy*, where it was printed in the April issue. Proudly, or perhaps egotistically, he hurried to Great Stuart Street to show off the printed review to Fleeming Jenkin, who read it then threw it on the floor contemptuously. 'That won't do,' he shouted at the startled Louis. 'You were thinking of yourself, not Salvini.' Stevenson knew he was right and perhaps recognised for the first time that 'life was not designed to minister to man's vanity'. That was his first and last drama critique.

Ever-perceptive, Fleeming Jenkin later remarked, 'Even if

you did act foolishly and worse than other men did, you did so from better motives.' It was Jenkin who introduced him to Japanese classical poetry, from which Stevenson extracted the lines he was to quote in 'Yoshida Torojiro'. They might have been his life-motif:

It is better to be crystal and be broken
Than to remain perfect as a tile upon the housetop.

When the formidable professor died suddenly at only fifty-three, Stevenson wrote his obituary for the *Academy*:

In talk he was active combative, pounced upon his interlocutors, and equally enjoyed a victory or a defeat. He had both wit and humour; had a great tolerance for men, little for opinions; gave much offence, never took any... He would not nurse a weakness in himself or you. He knew you and would not dissemble his knowledge; but you were aware he still loved you, and it was thus he desired you to return his affection; hand in hand, not gloved...

Just as poignantly fond was the simple postscript he added in a letter to Annie Jenkin: 'Dear me, what happiness I owe to both of you.'

(Coincidentally, Jenkin shared the same dates as one of Stevenson's great heroes, General Charles George 'Chinese' Gordon (1833–85). Stevenson never forgave Prime Minister Gladstone for not going to Gordon's rescue at Khartoum. When Gladstone was reported as 'never ceasing to talk about *Treasure Island*' when it first appeared in 1883, Stevenson retorted, 'He would be better attending England's imperial affairs.' Among the Stevenson memorabilia displayed at Vailima is General Gordon's last, desperate call for help, scrawled hurriedly, in Arabic, on a cigarette paper.)

If Stevenson's emerging literary personality and writing style was more English than Scots (and possibly more French than English), this was due to the influence of non-Scots like Fleeming Jenkin, Sidney Colvin and William Henley – especially the latter. Together with Bob Stevenson and Charles Baxter, these men comprised Stevenson's Praetorian Guard. They complemented the softer shield provided by the women in his life. There was always someone on hand. In this sense, his vulnerability was his very strength.

Now, in 1876, a new chapter of his life was about to begin. It started in the late summer when Walter Simpson invited him on a canoeing holiday on the canals between Antwerp and Grez-sur-Loing. Stevenson was happy to go along, thinking there might be another book in it (and there was: *An Inland Voyage*). What he didn't expect was that he would meet his future wife, 'the unique woman in the world', who was to combine the functions of both male guard and female protectress: Fanny Vandegrift Osbourne, a married American with two children – the future Mrs Robert Louis Stevenson.

Childhood must pass away, then youth,
as surely as age approaches.
The true wisdom is always to be seasonable,
and to change with a good grace
in changing circumstances.
CRABBED AGE AND YOUTH

CHAPTER FIVE

The Illogical Adventure

There is nothing like a bit of judicious levity.
ETHICAL STUDIES

HENLEY WAS RIGHT. Stevenson was never the same again after he met Fanny Osbourne. From that moment in 1876 his personality underwent a metamorphosis. His family and friends saw it happening before their very eyes and there was nothing they could do to stop it. It was as if he had been bewitched. He acted irrationally and out of character, and when everything settled again, the carefree Louis was gone. However, a determined, mature RLS emerged from the storm.

Frances Matilda Vandegrift was neither beautiful nor gifted, nor obviously exceptional. She wasn't even free to marry. But this was the woman who would unlock the passion in this only son of a sedate Edinburgh house and sweep him on his way to manhood. Born in Indianapolis, Indiana, on 10 March 1840, Fanny was of mixed Dutch and Swedish descent, with claims to a family connection with Captain Cook. Her father, Jacob Vandegrift, was a God-fearing merchant who dabbled in real estate. His wife, Esther was an equally devout Presbyterian. The grandmother who brought Fanny up unkindly said of her, 'God made her ugly', for the child's swarthy complexion had drawn rumours that her real mother was a Creole. As a girl she had shown a talent for drawing and a fondness for writing but was otherwise a complete tomboy, forever in trouble with her respectable family. No doubt they were relieved when, at seventeen, the vivacious young woman married the dashing twenty-year-old Lieutenant Samuel Osbourne, a Kentuckian who was then secretary to the Governor of Indiana. They were reckoned to be a good match and went on to have three children together: Isobel, in 1858; Samuel Lloyd, in 1868; and Hervey, in 1871. During the American Civil War of 1861–65 Sam was promoted to Captain, but he returned a changed man. His post-war wanderlust introduced Fanny to the nomadic life of a prospector's wife and in the mining camps she learned to shoot, swear and roll her own cigarettes. She coped with bandits, beggars, amorous miners and marauding Indians and knew what it was to set up home one day, only to pack it up again the next. For all his genuine fondness for his family, Sam was extremely unreliable and prone to serial infidelities. There were more and more quarrels and separations until Fanny eventually sought refuge in a hotel in San Francisco where she found work as a seamstress. Yet another reconciliation with Sam broke down and she went back to live with her parents in nearby Oakland. Much to their horror, she set up a rifle range in the back garden and held seances in the dining room.

Around this time she also began to take more serious interest in art and literature. Her daughter was already attending a school of design in San Francisco and when the idea of going to Europe together to study art was suggested by friends, it held a strong appeal to both women. Sam paid for the trip and in 1875 Fanny, Belle, Lloyd, Hervey and a hired governess set off for Europe.

Fanny and Belle had hoped to study at the Antwerp School of Art, but they arrived only to find that women were not admitted. At this juncture, Hervey fell ill. They travelled on to Paris, where Fanny and Belle enrolled at the Atelier Julian and lived an impoverished existence in a cheap rented apartment in Montmartre, subsisting on a diet of black bread and herring. Tragically, Hervey's condition deteriorated dramatically and Fanny was obliged to send for Sam. He arrived on 5 April 1876, just in time to see the little boy die from 'scrofulous tuberculosis'.

Hervey was buried in a pauper's grave in Saint-Germain cemetery. His agonising death marked Fanny as much as the war had affected her husband and she was never quite as vivacious thereafter. A few weeks later Sam left, having paid off all their bills, and given his wife enough to continue her art studies. Sam's payments to his family were erratic, but at this time he was enjoying one of his sudden bursts of affluence. Where did this money come from? Surely not from his wage as a court stenographer? Fanny did not inquire too closely.

Fearing for Lloyd's health and anxious to get away from the awful memories of Hervey's death, Fanny decided to take up the suggestion of a fellow American art student, who went by the name of Pardessus, and head for the artists' colony at Grez. The family was soon installed at the Hôtel Chevillon on the edge of the forest of Fontainebleau, only a day's coach-ride from Paris.

That summer, Stevenson outlined his own proposed Continental itinerary to Fanny Sitwell in a letter written at Swanston:

> To the Highlands first, to the Jenkins', then to Antwerp; thence, by canoe with Simpson, to Paris and Grez (on the Loing, and an old acquaintance of mine on the skirts of Fontainebleau) to complete our cruise next spring (if we're all alive and jolly) by Loing and Loire, Saône and Rhône to the Mediterranean. It should make a jolly book of gossip, I imagine.

The 'book of gossip' was to become *An Inland Voyage*, published in 1878. Soaked and cold, Stevenson paddled his canoe through all fifty-five locks between Brussels and Charleroi. It rained all the way. There were minor adventures and mishaps en route. At Pont-sur-Sambre, he and Simpson were mistaken for pedlars; at Landrecies, Stevenson drunkenly lectured the local judge on Scots law on illegitimacy; at Origny, he noted that 'the young ladies picked up their skirts as if they were sure they had good ankles'; at Moy he wrote, 'After a good woman, a good book and tobacco, there's nothing so agreeable on earth as a river.' Four days out of Chauney he was almost drowned 'to the immense regret of a large circle of friends and the permanent impoverishment of British Essayism and Reviewery', as he wrote to Henley:

> My boat calbutted me under a fallen tree in a very rapid current: and I was a good while before I got on to the outside of that fallen tree; rather a better while than I cared about.

At least it all made good copy. At Compiègne, which seemed to be occupied entirely by soldiers, he caught up with his mail; he was never to lose the excitement of opening a letter. They went on through Creil to Preçy and 'the worst inn in France'. By this time, for Stevenson at least, canoeing was beginning to pall and he was missing the intellectual and artistic stimulus he thrived on. He would sometimes strike ahead on his own; on one such occasion he was arrested at Chatillon for not having the correct papers and Walter had to bail him out. The incident was enough to convince both of them to lift their paddles out of the water.

> To the civilised man, there must come, sooner or later, a desire for civilisation. I was weary of dipping the paddle. I was weary of living on the skirts of life; I wished to be in the thick of it once more; I wished to get to work. I wished to meet people who understood my own speech, and could meet with me on equal terms, as a man and no longer as a curiosity.

For a man who had been a studied curiosity for most of his life, and who already spoke French 'like a Frenchman', this was an odd statement. What was true, however, was that he wanted to get out of that little boat, and, most of all, he wanted to get back to work. This was the real desire – and always would be:

> ... a man should have his life in his own pocket and never be thrown out of work by anything.

He worked, as he lived, a day at a time. Perhaps, with his health preoccupations it was the wisest thing to do:

> Anyone can carry his burden, however hard, until nightfall.
> Anyone can do his work, however hard, for one day. Anyone
> can live sweetly, patiently, lovingly, purely; till the sun goes
> down. And this is all that life really means.

But the same man also said:

> There is some life in humanity yet; and youth will now and
> again find a brave word in dispraise of riches, and throw up
> a situation to go strolling with a knapsack.

Somewhere between these three comments is the actual Robert
Louis Stevenson.

The waterlogged partners finally came back on land again and
took the train to Paris, where they were persuaded by Bob Stevenson to accompany him to Barbizon. At Siron's (now L'Hôtellerie du
Bas-Breau) they heard about the 'two beautiful Americans' at the
Chevillon and decided to investigate.

Legend has it that Stevenson fell in love with Fanny at his first
glimpse of her through the dining-room window of the hotel, and
she with him as he vaulted nimbly over the window sill to join her
party. Such a *coup de foudre* could not be further from the truth.

What is true, is that Fanny immediately fell for Bob, and he
fell in love with Belle. Stevenson himself was not immune to the
attractions of the eighteen-year-old, describing her as 'a bewitching
young girl, with eyes so large as to be out of drawing'. Belle was
already besotted by an Irish artist, Frank O'Meara. The atmosphere
at Grez was heady and intensely social, with bathing parties, lunch
parties, painting parties and drinking parties.

In the midst of all the carousing, Fanny and Stevenson discovered
a mutual affinity, on top of which she would have been impressed
by the fact that he was a published writer and reputedly heir to a
fortune. From the outset there was nothing sentimental about her

calculations where Stevenson was concerned. Stevenson later mentions her in admiring tones in a letter to his parents:

> One of the matrons was a very beautiful woman indeed; I played old fogey and had a great deal of talk with her which pleased me...

Behind the scenes, Bob, had sold Stevenson to Fanny as 'a real gentleman, whereas I'm rather a cad' – warding off any unwanted attentions and leaving him to concentrate on Belle. The flirtatious Belle was willing enough until she found that he had no real financial prospects; she then turned back to O'Meara, leaving Bob broken-hearted. In 1879, by which time he was married to someone else, he wrote to Stevenson:

> I think I would go through the rest of my career moderately content if I saw Belle once in a fortnight... and of course if she really took to me I would go for her.

Early in their acquaintance, Fanny described Stevenson as follows:

> The hysterical fellow who wrote the article about Belle, is a tall, gaunt, Scotsman with a face like Raphael, and between over-education and dissipation, has ruined his health, and is dying of consumption... [he] is heir to an immense fortune which he will never inherit. His father and mother, cousins, are both threatened with insanity, and I'm quite sure the son is. His article about Belle, as she says, was written for five pounds he wanted to give a pensioner of his that was in hospital.

The 'article about Belle' does not seem to have survived.

Fanny had never met anyone quite like Stevenson. His ability to laugh or cry at whim, to talk brilliantly without pause on everything and anything, or to burst into purple rages over nothing, all took a little getting used to. The spoiled brat was saved by the wit, the weakling by the charmer. It is hard to imagine a more unlikely pair. Birge Harrison, an American artist who met them at Grez, recalled:

> Mrs Osbourne was in no sense ordinary. Indeed she was gifted with a mysterious over-intelligence, which is almost impossible to describe, but which impressed itself upon everyone that came within the radius of her influence... She belonged to the quattrocento rather than the nineteenth century... Had she been born a Medici, she would have held rank as one of the most remarkable women of all time... The very antithesis of the gay, hilarious, open-hearted Stevenson, and for that reason perhaps the woman in all the world best fitted to be his life comrade and helpmate.

In *An Inland Voyage*, written after he had met Fanny at Grez, Stevenson opined, 'if a man finds a woman admires him, were it only for his acquaintance with geography, he will begin at once to build on that admiration'. He admired and was fascinated by Fanny, but there was no talk of love, let alone marriage. In various essays dating from this period, Stevenson expounded his views on the wedded state. In one, he says:

> A man becomes slack and selfish and undergoes a fatty degeneration of his moral being... if people married only when they fell in love, most of the world would die unwed.

And in another:

> Times are changed with him who marries; there are no more by-path meadows where you may innocently linger but the road lies long and dusty to the grave... to marry is to domesticate the recording angel...

And in yet another:

All women should marry, but no man should... And yet, when all has been said, the man who should hold back from marriage is in the same case with him who runs away from battle...

Falling in love was 'the one, illogical adventure, the one thing we are tempted to think of as supernatural in our trite and reasonable world'.

At the end of October, Fanny and her entourage returned to Paris. In early 1877, while staying with her in the rue Douay, Stevenson wrote an essay in which he took a rather dispassionate view of 'undying love':

When the generation has gone, when the play is over, when the thirty years' panorama has been withdrawn in tatters from the stage of the world, we may ask what has become of those great, weighty and undying loves... and they can only show us a few songs in a bygone taste, a few actions worth remembering and a few children who have retained some happy stamp from the disposition of their parents.

That was another thing – his own parents. He had been away for over a year and their letters pointedly suggested that he come home. His mother was apparently wasting away with missing him. His father reminded him that life was short ('at least mine is'). Meanwhile, Stevenson outlined Fanny's predicament in letters home, without stating how close they had become:

It is rather a pitiful story. She half-quarrelled with all her family to come over here and study art; and she can't do it, feels herself like a fish out of water in the life, and yet is ashamed to give in and go back.

However, in February 1877, he fell ill and had to return to Edinburgh whether he liked it or not. Fanny returned to Grez, where the living was cheaper. His mother and father welcomed their invalid home. Back in Edinburgh, Stevenson soon returned to health and again the tension with his father rose to the surface.

Although Stevenson hinted in a letter to Henley that there had been some dalliance with two of his old flames, the romance with Fanny was not over. That summer he returned to Grez. The plan was to share a canoe on the Loing.

> Deep, swift and clear, the lilies floated; fish
> Through the shadows ran. There thou and I
> Read kindness in our eyes and closed the match.

One doesn't need to read between the lines to see that the relationship was consummated during that visit.

> The hue of heather honey
> The hue of honey bees
> Shall tinge her golden shoulder
> Shall tinge her tawny knees.
> Dark as a wayside gypsy
> Lithe as a hedgewood hare
> She moves, a glowing shadow
> Through the sunshine of the fair;
> And golden hue and orange,
> Bosom and hand and head
> She blooms, a tiger lily
> In the snowdrifts of the bed.
> Tiger and tiger lily,
> She plays a double part,
> All women in the body,
> And all the man at heart.
> She shall be brave and tender,
> She shall be soft and high,
> She to lie in my bosom
> And he to fight and die.

He would certainly have to fight for her – against the bias of his parents, the prejudice of his friends and the inescapable fact that she was married already.

He returned again to Edinburgh, only to be 'whipped away to Penzance' on a gloomy family holiday which at least effected a fragile reconciliation with his father. Stevenson did not like Cornwall – 'It is not to my taste, being as bleak as the bleakest parts of Scotland and nothing like so pointed and characteristic.' The man who had been 'complaining about the cold since he was born' soon chafed to be back in chilly Edinburgh. However, he rejoined Fanny in Grez as soon as he could and on this visit news came that Bob had fallen ill. Stevenson persuaded Fanny to write to him, and one wonders why he didn't ask Belle to do so as well, given Bob's warm feelings for her. At any rate, Stevenson was no doubt preoccupied by his own swelling emotional symphony. The orchestration was complex. Stevenson was aware that decisions made now would affect the whole tempo of his future life.

It is not known what he said that caused Tom Stevenson to come immediately to France at his call. The Edinburgh father, who was so uncomfortable 'abroad' (which meant anything beyond the coastline of Scotland), who had called his son a 'humbug' for staying away from home so long, now spent days in Paris discussing the situation. Whether he visited Fanny at her new home on the rue Ravignan is not known, but one can be sure that she was mentioned. His son also provided another cause for concern – he dismissed the eye trouble he was having as 'a little bit of a nuisance', but acute opthalmia developed and, for a while, near-blindness threatened. However, the crisis appeared to pass and his father went home. Stevenson, still unwell, was taken into Fanny's apartment, but even with her experienced ministrations his condition worsened and by November she was so alarmed that she wrote asking Colvin to come and take him home. When Colvin could not oblige, she decided to take him to London herself.

As might be expected, she caused a sensation among Stevenson's friends. To Colvin, she brought to mind Napoleon with her indomitable determination; he described her eyes as being, 'full of sex and mystery'. Fanny Sitwell adored her free spirit. Henry James thought her 'primitive' and his sister called her 'barbarous', adding waspishly:

> From her appearance, Providence or Nature, whichever is responsible for her, designed her as an appendage to a hand organ... and so naked! Giving me the strangest feeling of being in the presence of an unclothed being.

By Christmas Stevenson was well again. Then, to everyone's surprise, especially his, Fanny decided to return to Grez with the still-ailing Bob Stevenson, determined to nurse him back to health as well. Stevenson crawled back to Edinburgh, discomfited by the pangs of rejection he was feeling. He was also perplexed to receive a letter from someone whom he described to Henley as:

> an enchanting young lady whom you have seen, or rather from her inspiration, threatening letters, exposure, etc.

We are told nothing more, and nothing more is heard of her.

After another miserable family holiday, at Gairloch on the Clyde, he described himself to one correspondent as a grieving widower. (Incidentally, at around this time he received his first piece of fan-mail – from a Mr A Patchett Martin in Australia.)

Already in low spirits, he heard from Bob that Fanny herself was 'not very bright in health'. This was an occurrence, or recurrence, of the mental illness that plagued her all her life, the price she paid, perhaps, for her reputed psychic gifts. All Stevenson knew was that she was down and he had to contrive to get to her without upsetting the family apple cart yet again. Fleeming Jenkin came to his rescue. He had been asked to be a juror at the Paris Exposition of 1878 and invited Stevenson to accompany him as his 'secretary' This was the cover he needed to get to Paris without rousing suspicions at Heriot Row. Stevenson did not enjoy playing a double game with his parents but the invitation was accepted with alacrity and by late spring he was back in Fanny's arms.

Stevenson must have been preoccupied as to how to resolve his emotional situation when, in June, the decision was made for him. Sam wrote ordering Fanny to bring his children back to the United States, and given her lack of independent finance, she probably felt she had no option but to return to her husband. Consequently, Fanny, Belle, Lloyd and Stevenson left for London together and Bob put them up at his house in Chelsea. On the day of their departure for the boat at Southampton, Bob took the Osbournes to Waterloo Station, with Stevenson turning up at the very last minute to make his farewells. There was time for only the briefest of exchanges before departure; as the train drew out of the station, Stevenson turned on his heel and walked down the platform without a backward glance.

*A happy man or woman is better
to find than a five-pound note.*
VIRGINIBUS PUERISQUE

CHAPTER SIX

A Steady Determination

The world was made before the English language,
and seemingly upon a different design.
TRUTH OF INTERCOURSE

PEOPLE NOW COME FROM all over the world to follow the route
Stevenson took through the Cévennes in the autumn of 1878. A
group from the Edinburgh Robert Louis Stevenson Club decided to
celebrate the 120th anniversary of the original tour. Their itinerary
was as follows:

Day 1 Le Monastier sur Gazelle to Le Bouchet-Saint-Nicolas
Day 2 Langogne.
Day 3 Cheylard l'Evêque
Day 4 La Bastide-Puylaurent
Day 5 Rogleton to Notre Dame des Nieges
Day 6 Le Bleymard
Day 7 To Le Pont de Montvert
Day 8 Florac
Day 9 Cassagnas
Day 10 Saint Germain de Calberte
Day 11 Saint Jean du Gard

This was one day longer than Stevenson took (from 22 September
until 2 October) but unlike Stevenson, they were sent off by a brass
band and led into each new halt by a piper. Evening entertainments
were provided by Stevenson bard John Shedden, and *they* enjoyed a
packed programme of exhibitions, lectures, dramatisations, recep-
tions and folk dancing.

Stevenson's largely solitary encounter with the mountain tracks
through the Cévennes involved the parallel inward journey of coming

to terms with his complicated emotions. After his difficult parting with Fanny in London on 15 August he had headed to Le Monastier, south of Le Puy, seeking the 'great solitude of four and twenty mountain hours'. He wrote to Charles Baxter on 17 September:

> I shall soon go off on a voyage for which I think I shall buy a donkey, and out of which, if I do not make a book, may my right hand forget its cunning.

He and his donkey, Modestine, 'travelled upwards of 120 miles, crossed several respectable ridges, and jogged along with [their] six legs by many a rocky and many a boggy by-road'. Modestine was bought for 65 francs and a glass of brandy two days after his letter to Baxter, and another two days after that, on a Sunday morning, he set out from Le Monastier 'as the bells were striking nine'.

> I travel not to go anywhere, but to go. I travel for travel's sake. The great affair is to move...

By keeping moving he discovered the working method which he would use, more or less continuously, until he settled in Samoa. From the Cévennes onwards, he would travel and observe, then write up his notes and add the finishing touches at leisure, and publish. Although it was to be an arduous, not to say anguished discipline at times, he kept at it, constantly preparing his pen for greater works to come. The publication of *Travels with a Donkey* in 1879 earned him thirty pounds and gained him a London literary agent, PG Hamerton. He was ready to start making his living from words.

His next project was a play, reflecting his continuing fascination with the stage from his childhood days with Skelt's cut-out figures toy theatre. As early as 1864 he had tried his hand at a drama based on the life of Edinburgh's very own cat-burglar, Deacon Brodie. It was put away 'in his coffer' until it was 'fished out' by Henley in 1878. While Stevenson was in the Cévennes,

Henley worked on it. On his return they decided to collaborate, and commenced that October at Swanston.

Henley had managed to convince Stevenson that their efforts would result in a money-spinner and intended the leading role for Henry Irving, but despite Henley's optimism and Colvin's attempts to use his influence on their behalf, the eminent actor-manager failed to bite. However, this first flirtation with Dame Theatre was an enjoyable gamble.

George Bernard Shaw (who regarded Irving as being 'fit for nothing but to be stuffed and mounted under glass to adorn the staircase of the Garrick Club') retrospectively observed in the *Saturday Review*:

> The real history of the drama in the last ten years is not in the prosperous enterprises of... Mr Irving, and the established West-End theatres but of the forlorn hopes led by... Messrs Henley and Stevenson and the rest of the Impossibilists.

Henley had hoped to break clear of Grub Street and his days of hack editing. But although he could talk a good play, he never dirtied his fingers with the mechanics of drama and Stevenson, for all his brilliance as a conversationalist, was undisputably at his best writing solo: while they both had excellent taste in theatre and knew a good effect when they saw it, their own playscripts were flat. Neither really had the vulgar fire of theatre in his belly. Henley's near-penury was chronic (until, late in life, when a Civil List pension brought some relief), and he often borrowed money from Louis, always with the assurance that he would pay it all back when the curtain went up on their hit play.

Stevenson left to visit Colvin at Trinity College, Cambridge, then went on to London where he wrote 'Providence and the Guitar', a short story about actors. In the comfort of the smoking room at the Savile Club he considered taking another walking tour, this time in England, but he hurt his heel and the plan was abandoned. Leslie Stephen suggested that he should write a novel. Instead, he started on another story for the *Cornhill*, 'Pavilion on the Links'.

He was missing Fanny. As if to compensate, he made much of his many friends. As Andrew Lang observed: 'Mr Stevenson possessed, more than any man I have ever met, the power of making other men fall in love with him'. Will Low similarly noted:

Fascination and charm are not qualities which Anglo-Saxon youths are prone to acknowledge, in manly avoidance of their supposedly feminising effect, but it was undoubtedly this attractive power which RLS held so strongly through life; and which, gentle though it be, held no trace of dependence or weakness.

Stevenson's own view was,

the best that we find in our travels is an honest friend. He is a fortunate voyager who finds many. We travel, indeed, to find them. They are the end and the reward of life. They keep us worthy of ourselves; and when we are alone, we are only nearer to the absent.

On his return to Edinburgh, he wrote 'Will o' the Wisp', a philosophical essay exploring issues of conscience and moral responsibility. In the spring of 1879, in a restless, melancholy mood, he again went back to London.

On the other side of the Atlantic, Fanny and Sam had moved to Monterey on the Californian coast, but the situation soon deteriorated and before long Sam abandoned the family yet again. Fanny lost no time in communicating her plight and Stevenson generous as ever, responded by sending her funds. There followed an intense correspondence and Fanny promised to seek a divorce. Stevenson was restless, and finding it difficult to work, returned to Scotland in a state of emotional turmoil. In Edinburgh he would at least be able to confide in Charles Baxter. His uneasiness about his own moral position at this time can been read between the lines of an essay he wrote deploring Robert Burns's 'Don Juanism'.

At the end of July a telegram from Fanny was delivered to Swanston. No one knows what it said, but Stevenson went straight to the office of the Anchor Line in Hanover Street and, at a cost of eight guineas, bought a ticket for New York. Set to leave in six weeks' time, he merely informed his parents that he would not be joining them for a proposed holiday at Gilsand Spa, as he had urgent business in London. He said no more than that, and felt terrible about it. Perhaps he rationalised that, given his uncertain state, the steamship reservation in his pocket was no guarantee that he would *actually* go.

His London friends were appalled at his decision but Stevenson would not be deterred. However, on Baxter's advice, he agreed to make a will. He tried to explain his position to Colvin: 'No man is of any use until he has dared everything. I feel just now as if I had, and so might become a man...'

As he wrote in *Lay Morals*:

let a man love a woman as far as he is capable of love, and for this random affection of the body there is substituted a steady determination which supersedes, adopts and commands all others.

Henley saw him off, wondering dolefully if he would ever see his friend again; and although he did, he always averred that the Louis he had known and loved departed on 7 August 1879, never to return.

Stevenson had hardly boarded the *Devonia* to begin the seventeen-day voyage between the Clyde and Sandy Hook, before his pen was in his hand and he was taking notes. His second class cabin was only a thin wall away from the penitentiary conditions inflicted on the luckless steerage passengers, trapped with their bedding and possessions in a compress of human misery. Stevenson's pen sizzled with fury and outrage – so much so, that his father actually blocked publication, paying publishers Kegan Paul to withdraw the book. Parts of the story appeared in signed instalments in *Longman's Magazine*, but *The Amateur ~Emigrant* was not published until 1895, a year after Stevenson's death, and even then in a bowdlerised form.

It was only half a man who disembarked at New York. Stevenson was always lean, but he came down the gangplank a wraith, and a drenched one at that, for the rain bucketed down. He made a bee-line for the first French restaurant he could find, in the hope that a meal and some good wine would put him to rights again. However, when he boarded the train at New Jersey his nightmare journey continued and he found he had exchanged 'discomfort for downright misery and danger'.

The *Devonia* had not been the only emigration ship to put in at New York that weekend: no less than three others had landed, each with a load of steerage hopefuls, all of whom seemed now intent on boarding the same west-bound train. Stevenson sat hemmed in for forty hours before he could stretch out on the wooden boards and try to sleep. What would he have given now for the *Devonia*'s 'slandicular cabin and the table playing bob-cherry with the ink bottle'. For eleven days he endured back-breaking conditions, comforted only by his sense of purpose. During the succession of dreadful, airless nights amidst the snoring and the swearing of his sweating fellow-passengers, he longed for morning with an intensity he had last known in Cummy's arms at a window in Heriot Row. With exhausted irony, he wrote to Colvin: 'I had no idea how easy it was to commit suicide. There seems nothing left of me; I died a while ago; I don't know who it is who is travelling'.

He attempted to distract himself, both from the present ordeal and future uncertainties by dipping into the six bulky volumes of Bancroft's *History of the United States* that he had brought with him. He later described his state of mind to Gosse:

I had no feeling one way or another, from New York to

California, until, at Dutch flat, a mining camp in the Sierra, I heard a cock crowing with a home voice, and then I fell into hope and regret both in the same moment.

Stevenson arrived in San Francisco three weeks after leaving Glasgow, a long three weeks by any standard, and he still faced the last lap.

Wearing a bowler hat and a new serge suit, with thirty pounds in his pocket, he made his way to Fanny's cottage in Alverado Street, Monterey. Fanny was shocked at his appearance (and it wasn't just the bowler hat). He, too, was in for an unpleasant jolt: although she was living apart from Sam, she had taken no steps to secure a divorce, as promised in their frenzied correspondence. Did she guess what he had undergone for her sake? Dismayed, he found a hotel and lived on cups of tea and laudanum, driven almost crazy by eczema. He was also put to the point of madness by Fanny's behaviour. She let it be known that her 'literary friend from Scotland has accepted an engagement to come to America and lecture'. This was not the engagement Stevenson had had in mind when he undertook his crucifying odyssey. To top it all, Sam Osbourne reappeared on the scene; after furtive discussions with Fanny, he took off again for San Francisco; shortly after that, Fanny herself left for Oakland.

With nothing to hold him in Monterey, Stevenson decided to hire a horse and wagon and take to the hills, quitting the 'melancholy fogs' of the coast for the drier, warmer climate of the Carmel Valley in the Santa Lucia mountains. As the path wound higher he eventually had to leave the wagon. He loaded up the horse and pressed on – taking his itch, his troubled mind, his wrecked body and his broken heart with him.

An aim in life is the only fortune
worth the finding; and it is not
to be found in foreign lands,
but in the heart itself.
THE AMATEUR EMIGRANT

CHAPTER SEVEN

Marriage *in extremis*

Hope, they say, deserts us at no period of our existence.
From first to last, and in the face of smarting disillusions,
we continue to expect good fortune, good health, and
good conduct; and that so confidently, we judge
it needless to deserve them.
VIRGINIBUS PUERISQUE

MOVING FURTHER UP ROBINSON CANYON each day, writing a little as he went, Stevenson stumbled on until his body forced him to stop. This was a different thing altogether from the Cévennes. The coughing became worse, cold sweats broke out and utter inertia set in. He could barely summon the energy to water his horse. He staggered with the water bucket, spilling most of it. One night, by the San Clemente Creek, he felt dizzy. The mountain tops seemed to swirl around his head and the last thing he remembered was the sound of tinkling bells...

The next morning he was discovered unconscious under a tree by a goat-herd, Jonathan Wright (the bells Stevenson had heard belonged to his goats). Somehow the herd got him back to his partner's ranch-house and there Anson Smith and his family nursed him for over two weeks. 'Captain' Smith, as he was called, was rough but kindly and his children thought the unexpected house guest a rare novelty. Full of gratitude, Louis set abou teaching the young Smiths to read almost as soon as he began to recover.

One day, he had a visitor. It was Timothy Rearden, Fanny's trusted lawyer whom she had sent to reclaim her 'Scotch friend'; her emissary brought the news that she was at last prepared to initiate a private divorce. Rearden (with whom Fanny had had a long, flirtatious friendship), doubtless wondered at first what on earth she saw in this human wreck, though he soon succumbed to Stevenson's charm. It was clear that the Scotsman needed professional medical attention. And so, with the help of the goat-herds, the gaunt figure was gently brought back to Monterey. Lloyd recalled his arrival there:

> He looked ill even to my childish gaze; the brilliancy of his eyes emphasised the thinness and pallor of his face. His clothes, no longer picturesque but merely shabby, hung loosely on his shrunken body.

Fanny wanted to take Louis into her own home immediately, but Rearden cautiously advised her to observe the proprieties rather than risk compromising the divorce. Stevenson was therefore moved into a 'dismal room' in the old adobe called The French Hotel (now known as Stevenson House), in Houston Street. Jules Simoneau's bistro nearby became his social hub. A routine soon developed of walks to the Alverado Street post office to collect his mail, followed by morning coffees that often lingered on into long lunches. He enjoyed the rather cosmopolitan company he found there– Bronson, the local newspaper editor (who subsidised Stevenson by paying for a series of articles the paper couldn't afford), Adolpho Sanchez (Nellie Vandegrift's fiancé) and a Dr Heintz. Jules Simoneau was a gregarious character, always delighted to meet up with anyone who could speak French, play chess and discuss the world beyond the Monterey peninsula, likened by Stevenson to 'a dissenting chapel on a wet Sunday'.

By now Stevenson regarded himself as morally, if not officially, engaged to Fanny. Then Sam suddenly reappeared on the scene, thoroughly disconcerting Fanny, who promptly fell ill again, her sight and hearing being alarmingly affected. Her illness galvanised Stevenson into a direct discussion of his intentions with Sam, who declared he had no objection to their marrying, as long as they observed 'a reasonable time' after the divorce, set to come through in January. He even loaned Fanny some money to pay for the wedding.

Fanny went back to East Oakland to recover and prepare for her second essay at matrimony. Stevenson remained in Monterey, 'a lovely place, which I am growing to love'. After Christmas he left for San Francisco to be near Fanny. There was still no word from his parents and the strain was telling. He wrote anxiously to Baxter:

Now, for God's sake, about my father? Tell me please, Charles. Since I have gone away I have found out for the first time how much I love that man; he is dearer to me than all except F.

It was important to resume good relations with his parents for several reasons, not least because he was almost out of money. He feared that his father would find it hard to forgive him for running off with hardly a word.

Belle was now married to an artist, Joe Strong, and Louis initially stayed with them in New Montgomery Avenue, in the Latin Quarter of San Francisco. Then suddenly he moved out, and into Mrs Carson's Boarding House in Bush Street. He wrote elliptically to Colvin:

No more to Strong, difficulties about Belle having hurt me a good deal. More hell with that young lady...

It is hard to know what was really going on. Did Louis remind Belle too much of his cousin, and her great admirer, Bob Stevenson? Or, as Katherine Durham (Lloyd Osbourne's first wife) claimed, did Belle herself want to marry Louis in order to get free from Joe Strong, and in fact asked him to do so? This suggestion is generally dismissed as preposterous, but it would account for his leaving the Strong household as hurriedly as he did.

Belle certainly did not perceive that her prospective stepfather had an irresistible passion for her mother:

> Lou's conduct was not that of a romantic lover who had
> followed a sweetheart halfway round the world... he was
> almost coldly casual towards my mother... and maybe she
> saw in this contrast to my father the security from infidelity
> that had wrecked his marriage...

Fanny, however, was anxious to show Stevenson off, as long as
the scrutiny was not too wearing. She did not want their marriage
bed to be another sick-bed. She introduced him to friends, including
Dora and Virgil Williams and Charles Warren Stoddard, who had
just come back from the South Seas full of intriguing traveller's
tales.

At this juncture, Sam Osbourne sent word that he had lost his
job and could offer no further financial support. Despite his own
non-existent financial resources (he was living on a two-bit lunch
in the middle of the day), Stevenson immediately assumed the duty
of provider. As he wrote to Colvin, 'I... who have made so poor a
business of my life am now about to embrace the responsibility for
another.' And not just for Fanny – but for her son, her sister, three
horses, two dogs and five cats. Stevenson asked Baxter to sell some
books from his library to raise funds. Baxter immediately sent him
fifty pounds, pointing out that he could have all the money he needed
if he would just come home again. As things stood, Stevenson was
running a serious risk of being disinherited.

Just as he was bracing himself for the big day, he was struck
down with a haemorrhage while looking after his landlady's
consumptive son. He felt ghastly even conceding, 'I must own
the guts are a little knocked out of me'. This was the first visit of
'Bluidy Jack', and for his remaining fourteen years his worries would
more often than not be spelt out in blood. The doctor diagnosed
'galloping consumption', possibly a contagion from the Carson
boy. Fanny moved into urgent action. After installing him briefly
in a hotel, she decided to defy convention by taking him into her

home where she nursed him night and day till he pulled back from the abyss. He would later say lightly, 'I fear I must be a vain man, for I thought it a pity I should die'. By now, Stevenson was utterly committed to Fanny ('The Vice', as Henley dubbed her), however difficult their circumstances, as he wrote to Gosse:

> I am having a rough time here... a combination of lapsing money, horrid feuds with threatening letters, telegrams requesting me to come home right away because my father was ill... and doctors telling me here that those who are most dear to me would not last the night. Your letter was like a warm shake of the hand in the midst of all these concerns... Gosse, I am trying to behave well, and in some sort, which is as much as one can say, succeeding.

Note the cryptic 'I am trying to behave well'. At the end of April, a cable arrived from his father:

> HEREWITH ADVANCE DRAFT 250 POUNDS STERLING. COUNT ON SAME PER ANNUM.

Baxter must have said something. The reconciliation was a lifesaver, in every sense. The first thing Stevenson did with the cash was to go to the dentist and get new teeth. It was such an American thing to do. His cabled reply read:

> THIS IS TO INFORM YOU THAT THE AMERICAN EAGLE IS COMING – THE AMERICAN EAGLE I SAY – THE BRITISH LION BRINGS YOU THIS WARNING.

Fanny's divorce finally came through and they were at last free to marry. A date was set for 19 May. (Was either of them, one wonders, aware of the old saw, 'Marry in May and rue the day'?)

Stevenson was now writing up *The Amateur Emigrant*. He dedicated it to Robert Alan Mowbray Stevenson.

Our friendship was not only founded before we were born by a community of blood, but is in itself near as old as my life... Although we may not be old in the world, we are old to each other.

Bob wrote from England, wishing him well in his marriage. It was not a happy letter. His own marriage had failed and he was clearly still in love with Belle:

How much our elders deceived us in saying that the pleasures of the senses were the most deceptive and misleading... I never think of Belle or look at letters or anything, yet really I am always conscious of her...

Stevenson was writing *A Vendetta in the West*. The novel's central character, perhaps based on Fanny when she was Belle's age, or on Belle herself, never reached completion and the project was dropped as suddenly as it had been taken up. He went back to the essay form, dictating to Nellie Sanchez.

The wedding day arrived. The Reverend William Scott performed the Presbyterian ceremony in his own home at 521 Post Street; Dora Williams undertook to be the witness. 'She was our Best Man and Bridesmaid rolled into one, and the only third of the wedding party,' said Stevenson. The wedding certificate gives his age as thirty, although he was merely in his thirtieth year. Fanny's age is set down as forty. She is described as 'widowed', based on a mistaken rumour that Sam had been scalped by Indians. The wedding lunch at the Viennese Bakery was a distinctly subdued occasion.

It was not my bliss I was interested in when I was married, it was a sort of marriage *in extremis*; and if I am where I am, it is thanks to the love of that little lady who married me when I was a mere complication of cough and bones...

Not long after the wedding he wrote to his brother-in-law, Jacob:

I know I am on trial; if I can keep well till next winter, I have every reason to hope [for] the best. But on the other hand, I may very well never see next spring. In view of this I am all the more anxious she should see my father and mother; they are well off, thank God, and even suppose that I die, Fanny will be better off than she had much chance of being otherwise...

And to his mother:

Doubtless she is not the daughter-in-law you have always pictured, but nor is she the scarlet woman you fear. She is my wife, and if you can love my wife, it will, I believe, make me love her and you the better.

Fanny enclosed a photograph with her first letter to Tom Stevenson:

Please remember that my photograph is flattering; unfortunately all photographs of me are... Louis thinks me the most beautiful creature in the world... It is because he loves me... I do so earnestly hope that you will like me...

The honeymoon was in the Napa Valley in the company of twelve-year-old Lloyd and Chuchu, the dog. Stevenson made a great fuss of Lloyd, who later vividly recollected the occasion was present at the Hot Springs Hotel in Calistoga when Stevenson took his first-ever telephone call. He did not enjoy the experience, much to Lloyd's amusement. One wonders, who was at the other end of that historic conversation? Probably a desk clerk. Stevenson developed an ongoing love-hate relationship with hotel desk clerks.

As one drives through the Napa Valley today, huge hoardings displaying Stevenson's likeness announce that you are in 'Stevenson Wine Country'. Certainly the first impression Stevenson himself had of the place was of wine – eighteen bottles of it. His family were guests at the vineyard owned by Jacob Schram, one of the original Silverado Squatters. Schram offered Louis unlimited access to his cellar, much to Fanny's annoyance. She happened to mention her husband's need to get away from the muggy Californian coastline to another guest, Morris Friedberg, who recommended a miner's shack two thousand feet up the south-eastern slope of Mount Helena. Fanny did not hesitate. Two days later, they were there.

They found a dilapidated building covered with weed and half-buried in debris. Fanny immediately set about licking it into shape and on their first night, Stevenson had a bath by candle-light. She was in her pioneering element, full of ingenuity; she even fashioned door hinges out of an old boot. Gradually Stevenson began to recuperate in the cold, dry air. If he couldn't hold a hammer he could wield a pen. Sitting up in bed, he kept at his writing and produced *The Silverado Squatters*. A more substantial work than his previous travel essays, it is hard to believe that it was written in such primitive conditions.

> Our day was not very long but it was very tiring. To trip along unsteady planks, or wade among shifting stones, to go to and fro for water, to clamber down the glen to the Toll House for meat and letters, to cook, to make fires and beds, were all exhausting to the body.

Stevenson writes as if he did all these things. Probably at most he would light the fire, or, always hungry for letters, go down for the mail. He developed writer's cramp, Fanny smashed her thumb with a hammer and Lloyd fell ill with diphtheria. The mountain air came at too high a price. With no little relief, they came back down the mountain to Calistoga where Joe Strong had come to meet them with a stage-coach full of people, including Belle and Nellie. They had an impromptu party there by way of farewell to Silverado.

Stevenson had come to the point of return. The journey that had begun at St Pancras Station almost a year before had ended, and it was time to go back. Fanny wrote to her mother-in-law:

Now, at last, I think we may venture to make the journey without fear, though every step must be made cautiously. I am sure now he is on the high road to recovery and health, and I believe his best medicine will be the meeting with you and his father, for whom he pines like a child...

She knew exactly the right thing to say to ensure a warm welcome.

The return train journey from San Fransisco could not have been more different from Louis's outward trip. It was first-class all the way. He came into his own over cocktails and cigarettes; the same appears to have been true on the first-class Atlantic crossing in the *City of Chester*, which landed at Liverpool on 17 August 1880. Colvin was so eager to see Stevenson again that he went out in the packet to meet him on board, while Tom and Margaret waited on the dockside. Their son introduced Fanny with the words: 'My wife has done me the honour of divorcing her husband in order to marry me'. Fanny gave them her best smile and extended both hands. It was as if she were spreading her wings.

We fall in love, we run to and fro upon the earth like frightened sheep. And now you are to ask yourself, when all is done, would you not have been better to sit by the fire at home and be happy thinking?
WALKING TOURS

CHAPTER EIGHT

Child of Air

No baggage, that was the secret of existence.
THE WRECKER

IN THE SILVERADO SQUATTERS Stevenson wrote:

I am a Scotchman, touch me and you will find the thistle; I am a Briton, and live and move and have my being in the greatness of our national achievements; but am I to forget the long hospitality of that beautiful and kind country, France? or has not America done me favours to confound my gratitude... ?

His Scottishness was always with him, yet no sooner had he returned to his homeland than he was longing to get away again. He was quick to use his valetudinarian excuse – 'Another winter here would kill me' – to leave as soon as he could. 'I must flee from Scotland. For me, it is the mouth of the pit.' Basic good manners, however, prevented his leaving too soon after his return.

Baxter, like Henley, saw at once that the old Louis was no more, and that Fanny was the difference. Stevenson himself admitted:

I got my little finger into a steam press called the 'Vandegrifter' and my whole body and soul had to go in after it. I came out as limp as a lady's novel.

For her part, Fanny was thoroughly enjoying the sensation she was causing in Heriot Row. She was 'milking it', as actors say. The servants in the house were astounded. 'The young maister has merrit oan till a black wummin,' said one. 'But she smokes,' said

89

a guest, aghast. To which Tom Stevenson calmly replied 'So do I'. He was bowled over by his exotic American daughter-in-law, and thought she spoke excellent English – 'for a foreigner'. Louis had used words like 'peepy' and 'dowie' to describe her: old Scots words that indicate an inner melancholy. That she was putting on such an act for his parents would not have surprised him, for he knew her as 'a woman not without art'. His mother would probably have agreed.

In her unruffled Edinburgh way Margaret Stevenson was polite and hospitable to her guest, but she saw the game the younger woman was playing. 'It was quite amusing,' she said, 'how entirely she agreed with my husband on all things.' Her brother, George Balfour, had similar misgivings about this addition to the family. He told Tom frankly that Fanny was a besom, adding quickly 'I married a besom myself and I have never regretted it.' Tom, for his part, was relieved she was no worse than she was, and thought her 'a sensible wee body.'

Fanny was too wise to go too far with 'Uncle Tom', as she called him. As the corner-stone of the Stevenson fortune, he was someone who had to be cultivated. That apart, she genuinely liked and admired him. Tom Stevenson was a complicated man and although his wife seemed altogether more obvious, her daughter-in-law guessed she had more sides than she presented. If Tom was the key to the coffers, Fanny knew instinctively that Margaret was the key to a fuller understanding of her son.

Meanwhile, her own son, Sam, (now always called Lloyd) could only have been bewildered by the subtle game-playing of the adults. He took refuge in his stepfather's company – 'Lulu', in his essential personality, was hardly older than twelve himself.

Severe catarrh was now added to Stevenson's catalogue of ills and it was decided to take a holiday at the Ben Wyvis Hotel in Strathpeffer before winter set in. Louis enjoyed the Highland scenery well enough but had to brace himself to face his fellow-tourists. He hated tourists anywhere. 'ogres', he called them, and there seemed to be plenty in Strathpeffer. The Stevensons could not stay long in any case: Louis had an appointment in Edinburgh with his uncle Dr George Balfour. Balfour diagnosed tuberculosis and recommended a stay in a sanatorium in Switzerland. In the first week of October they were on a train once more, bound for Dr Karl Ruedi's clinic in Davos.

Their stop-over in London was the occasion of a boozy lunch in Stevenson's honour at the Savile, which flowed on well into the afternoon. He relished being the centre of attention, joking that it was only because of his new American teeth. The old mischief was in him yet. Fanny felt shut out and took her revenge by spending Tom Stevenson's money like water, assisted by Lloyd, who was working hard to develop expensive tastes. The week in London put a dent in their finances and widened the divide between Stevenson's new wife and his old friends. Henley made no secret of his dislike – or was it jealousy? He considered Fanny to have little poise and no class. Her novelty gave her no particular purchase among the Savile circle. She was frozen into social impotence. Stevenson made little show of being gallant; as he would admit, 'my wife is everything that is irritating in a woman, but without her I am nothing'. How often that phrase, 'I am nothing' was to resound in the family: Margaret would say it of herself without her son, Fanny of herself without her husband, but Stevenson said it first – of Fanny.

In *Virginibus Puerisque* he wrote, 'marriage puts old friends to the door', but that was hardly evident so far. Some of his closest friends would never be reconciled to his relationship with Fanny but at least all concerned recognised and honoured the fact that his love of writing took precedence over all else.

London must have taken its toll on Fanny. As soon as they arrived in Davos, she fell sick. Stevenson, on the other hand, with his perennial look of 'blasted boy, blighted youth', came to life among the snows. On their arrival on 7 November the porter at the Hotel Belvedere mistook Fanny for his mother, much to Stevenson's amusement but not to hers. She took to her room and sulked. Louis and Lloyd tactfully kept out of her way and took their dog on a walk. They saw 'a few more invalids marching to and fro upon the snow or skating on the ice rink… even the shopkeepers were consumptive'.

> It was a world of black and white – black pine woods and white snow… the place is half-English to be sure… but it still remains half-German… the row of sunburned faces can present the first surprise… in the rare air, clear cold, and blinding light… a man is stingingly alive… you can cast your shoe over the hill-tops.

Despite the exhilarating scenery, life under Dr Ruedi's regimen soon palled. The social environment was altogether too sterile for Stevenson, though he made an effort to participate in the silly games and pursuits of the other patients. But the superficial normality of the situation would evaporate when someone didn't turn up for breakfast the following morning and their place setting would be discreetly removed. Stevenson did get on with the head waiter – an avid reader – and in his unflappable way he penetrated the various cliques, causing gossip and murmurs wherever he went. He even played billiards. A fellow-patient, Harold Vallings, reported that:

> The balls flew wildly about, on or off the table as the case might be; but seldom indeed ever threatened a pocket or got within a hair's breadth of a cannon.

Stevenson's only comment was, 'What a fine thing a game of billiards is – once a year or so.' Another patient noticed that

> a crowd would always kindle him… On one occasion he read, at an entertainment given in the hotel drawing room, Tennyson's 'Lucknow', but he did not impress his audience, as he was thought too theatrical and rather stagey. He had the temperament of a reciter rather than a reader and was perhaps too impassioned and histrionic for the sober-minded.

He found some intellectual consolation visiting the author John

Addington Symonds: he appreciated the Scot's playfulness with themes and ideas, while Stevenson matched his learning with sheer conversational daring, 'illuminated by unforeseeable caprices of humour and fantasy', as Colvin put it.

Stevenson was trying to write a history of the Scottish Highlands, but couldn't settle to any decent work. 'I have no style and cannot write,' he complained. Essays were begun and left unfinished. Davos felt like a cage – 'the mountains are about you like a trap... you live in holes and corners, and can change only one for the other'. Fanny seemed to have lost all her energy. Surrounded as he was by the sick and the imminently dying, Stevenson began to fear for himself.

They also had to provide Lloyd with some education. A tutor was hired and Stevenson encouraged the boy to work with the little printing press he had brought with him from California. Lloyd turned out menus for the local hotels and Stevenson did some woodcuts, adding matching verses. Published by Chatto and Windus in 1899 as *A Stevenson Medley*, for the most part these were the trivial output of a frustrating period. He read Dickens, an author he did not admire, just to pass the time. Sheer boredom was pressing down hard on all three of them. Even though Dr Ruedi said that another year at Davos would definitely improve his condition, by mid-April they had packed Lloyd off to a church boarding school in Bournemouth and departed for Siron's Inn in Barbizon.

Nor did they stay long *there*. Fanny had a sudden suspicion of cholera from the open drains around the inn, and in no time they were in Paris, at the Hôtel St Romain on the rue Saint-Hoch. In the early hours of one morning, Stevenson endured another haemorrhage. A week in Paris had reduced him to 'the limpness peculiar to that of a kid-glove'. Funds were running low again – although this did not prevent Fanny from scouring antique shops. They had to move to cheaper accomodation before they were rescued by a generous money order from Scotland. It was the end of May 1881 and Edinburgh beckoned again.

Margaret Stevenson arranged an immediate decampment to the Scottish Highlands, where she and Tom had taken the summer lease of Kinnaird Cottage in Pitlochry, which came with Mrs Sims and her daughter as live-in help. The plain food and comfortable accommodation did them all good. The only problem was the Scottish weather. It rained without stop, day after day. Cooped up by the fire most of the time, Stevenson started 'The Body-Snatcher', based on the Edinburgh murderers, Burke and Hare but laid it aside after a while, 'in justifiable disgust, the tale being horrid' – in favour of what turned out to be a masterpiece of a short story in Scots, 'Thrawn Janet'.

He now took the notion to apply for the Chair of History and Constitutional Law at Edinburgh University, which involved only three months of lecturing during the summer and carried a reasonable stipend. Tom Stevenson, who came up to Pitlochry at weekends, may have seen the advert in *The Scotsman*; the decision may have been influenced by something that Symonds had said at Davos about Stevenson's not being a university man – not a thorough one, at any rate. Whatever the reason, his ambitions were suddenly academic, and, supported by references from willing but astonished friends, he formally applied for the Chair.

To no one's surprise, except his own, he received only nine votes against his opponent's hundred plus. Fanny was delighted. She had no desire for university life: she had had her fill of intellectuals. To offset her son's disappointment, Margaret Stevenson moved the whole lot of them further north to another Highland cottage, in Braemar in Aberdeenshire. The rain followed them. To amuse Lloyd, who was frustrated by having to remain indoors for so long each day, Stevenson embarked on the boy's story that was to make his name. It all began with Lloyd drawing a map of an island 'with the aid of pen and ink and a shilling box of water-colours'. Stevenson joined in, using his memory of Hugh and Alan Stevenson to create an imaginary island where treasure was hidden. The idea of buried treasure came from a rumour he had heard in Monterey that someone had dug up some old coins. The name Juan Silverado, from *The Silverado Squatters*, became John Silver, the story's leading character. The resemblance between that 'tall man with a face like a ham and only one leg' and a certain William Henley was more than coincidental. Stevenson told him:

> It was the sight of your maimed strength and masterfulness that begot John Silver. Of course he is not in any other quality or feature the least like you; but the idea of the maimed man, ruling and dreaded by the sound, was entirely taken from you.

It was while writing *Treasure Island* that Stevenson took to reading out his day's work after the evening meal. His listeners commented at the effectiveness of his speaking voice and although Fanny disliked the story, she loved hearing him read it. In a wonderful surge of just fifteen September days, 'by the cheek of a brisk fire with the rain drumming on the windows', Stevenson completed the map and finished more than half the text. He entitled it *The Sea Cook* and began to wonder where he would place it.

This was decided for him when Alexander Japp visited with Colvin and Gosse, and heard one of the nightly readings. Stevenson had invited Japp to come to Braemar to discuss certain criticisms he had made of something he had written. Japp, completely disarmed by Stevenson, returned to London bearing the unfinished *Sea Cook* and showed it to James Henderson, editor of *Young Folks*. Henderson disliked the title, but loved the story and accepted it for serialisation. This meant that Stevenson now had to finish it.

He had gone dry at Chapter Sixteen. At Braemar he could not summon up the inspiration to continue. He tried again in Edinburgh, and again in Weybridge, Surrey, while visiting George Meredith. With Fanny and Lloyd he returned to Davos for the winter, taking the parcel of pages with him. They rented the Chalet am Stein and there Stevenson finally completed his sun-filled story in another momentous fifteen-day burst:

> Down I sat one morning to the unfinished tale, and behold! it flowed from me like small talk... and again at the rate of a chapter a day, I finished it.

The parcel was duly sent back to Henderson who ran it in *Young Folks* under the title by which all know it, *Treasure Island*. While the serial was running, Stevenson sought his father's help in preparing it as a book. Tom was delighted to assist – it was good therapy for both of them – and eventually, through Henley's good offices, it was published by Cassell and Company. Stevenson got a hundred pounds for his work, 'a hundred jingling, tingling, golden, minted quid – a deal more than it's worth'.

Henley refused the commission due to him for placing the manuscript, and it is unlikely that Stevenson senior received anything for his input, which included helping to redraw the map of the treasure island after the publishers lost the original. (Stevenson was devastated – 'Somehow it wasn't the same Treasure Island to me'.)

The mendacious Lloyd Osbourne, who was not at hand when it got really hot in the literary kitchen, was later to boast that if it hadn't been for his toy box of paints, *Treasure Island* would never have been written. It became a classic in his life-time. Why wasn't he just content to live on the generous royalties it gave him?

An abortive writing exercise begun around this time was *The Squaw Man*, which soon joined *A Vendetta in the West* in the waste-paper basket. Stevenson had resumed his friendship with Symonds and joined with him in translating the Latin poets into English. A pencil and notebook went with him everywhere, the words continued to be put down and gradually polished into articles, poems, short stories and novels. When he was not writing, he was talking; when not talking, he was reading. Words, in one form or another, were his *raison d'être*.

At least the pure air of Davos agreed with him, even if most of his fellow patients did not. Fanny hated it. She fell ill and departed to seek medical care in Zürich, taking Lloyd out of school to accompany her. On their return, Stevenson went to meet them at Berne, enduring a seven-hour sleigh-ride each way to do so. Fanny was as irascible as ever. Stevenson was both concerned and irritated – 'I wish to God, I or anybody knew what was the matter with my wife.'

To add to his domestic complications, Lloyd refused to go back to school in Bournemouth and another expensive tutor had to be engaged. Belle wrote from San Francisco complaining that Louis wasn't sending enough money. One wonders how much irony laced the letter he sent her on November 1880 from the Hotel Belvedere: 'May coins fall into your coffee, and the finest wines and wittles lie smilingly about your path. Your dear Papa, RLS.' She obviously took him at his word, making repeated demands for cash thereafter from 'Lulu', her provider.

Stevenson had to cope with all this while trying to get on with his work. No wonder there were rows with Fanny – loud, flaming rows. Servants came and went with telling regularity. Fanny couldn't cope with servants. She wasn't used to them. Her solution, as ever, was to keep moving. But where to now? They returned to London in the spring of 1882 to meet up with the elder Stevensons who had travelled from Scotland especially to discuss the situation. Stevenson again attended Sir Andrew Clark, whom he had seen in 1873. Then, the doctor had ordered Stevenson south, but now he ordered him north.

Stevenson had hardly arrived at their rented cottage in Kingussie on Speyside when he had a bad haemorrhage. Unfortunately, Fanny fell ill at the same time. Stevenson returned to London and another appointment with Clark, who now suggested warm sea air. To Stevenson, that meant the South of France. He persuaded Bob, who was at a loose end and in low spirits, to go as well. What a contrast they made to the cousins who had stormed through France in 1878, 'bent on art and the pleasures of the flesh'. Louis suffered another two haemorrhages at Montpellier. Between these bouts, sometime in October 1882, he wrote a very serious letter to Fanny:

I am a very low horrid fellow... I do not ask you to love me any more. I am too much trouble. Besides, I thought myself all over last night; and, my dear, such rubbage [*sic*]. You cannot put up with such a man... I hear from you very rarely... you might write oftener, I think...

There is no note of Fanny's reply.

After Bob returned to London, Louis went on to Marseilles. Perhaps it was beginning to dawn on him that his wife was not the constant carer he had hoped for. Here he was, looking after her. Time, perhaps, to reconsider their bargain. He was obviously not her first priority. Lloyd was number one, Belle number two, Nellie, her sister, came next, and he would appear to share fourth place with the dog. Just as he was considering the situation, Fanny pre-empted any action he might have taken by joining him in Marseilles. He wrote to his mother, 'The wreck was towed into port yesterday evening.' Fanny had trumped him again.

There's an old Scottish song which begins, 'There's nae luck aboot the hoose, there's nae luck at a''. There certainly seemed to be no luck about Campagne Defli, their latest address. They should have guessed there was a catch, with such a low rent, but Fanny was in and hanging up pictures before he knew where he was. His letter seems to have stung her into something of her old action, though now she went as warily with her husband as she did with his father. Stevenson crawled into bed as soon as it was set in place, hoping all would be well. No such luck. The haemorrhages continued and when a typhoid outbreak threatened Marseilles, Fanny whipped him off to Nice, where they were joined by Lloyd. Stevenson hadn't the strength to deny her, and let himself be transplanted to the Grand Hotel.

Strangely enough, at this nadir he produced the poems that became *A Child's Garden of Verses*. Possibly these were prompted by his experiments with woodcuts on Lloyd's toy printing-press at Davos. Perhaps thoughts of childhood were triggered by his concern for his cousins Bob and Katharine, his favourite childhood companions at Colinton Manse. At any rate, Stevenson was always a full inhabitor of his own childhood, with all its demons; he had to write it out to be rid of it. That is, if he wanted to be rid of it.

> But do not think you can at all
> By knocking on the window, call
> That child to hear you. He intent

Is still on his play business bent.
He does not hear, he will not look,
Nor let be lured out of this book.
For long ago, the truth to say,
He is grown up and gone away;
And it is but a child of air
That lingers in the garden there.

There was little time for lingering now. As usual, Fanny expressed her American 'right' to the pursuit of happiness through an obsessive quest for the perfect place to live. Her husband's health was always presented as the justification, but in fact she was a driven, disturbed woman, plagued by imagined health threats. She dissolved into needless panic in the belief that typhoid was sweeping the Riviera. Stevenson managed to terminate the long lease they had taken on Campagne Defli, and now they considered Cannes, St Raphaël and Lake Geneva. In March 1883, Fanny found Châlet la Solitude, situated on the steep hill between old Hyères with its Saracen fortress and the new town on the plain below – in that respect, reminiscent of Edinburgh. For RLS, it was love at first sight.

The same may have applied to Valentine Roch, their new Swiss maid, who was young, efficient and attractive. She also had a sense of humour which she shared with her master, if not with her mistress. Nicknamed 'Joe' by Stevenson, she was soon the hub of the household. Fanny realised she had made a mistake and made life intolerable for the girl, but Valentine was made of stronger stuff than Fanny imagined. She nursed Stevenson through a dangerous flu. When she then succumbed herself, Fanny nursed her and a truce was declared. Stevenson positively purred with contentment. He had his hair cut short, grew a little beard so that he looked more French, and settled down to work, always the best medicine. Gratifyingly, he was beginning to make his literary name, and an income – 'This year I shall pass three hundred pounds.' It was time to concentrate.

Stevenson's Hyères days followed a uniform pattern: at his desk all morning; a stroll in the afternoon; letters, and a nap before dinner; good talk round the table, with good wine. Then to bed with a book to prepare the mind for tomorrow. It was indeed idyllic, and it had its moments, as one of his poems suggests. He gave the title in decorous Latin, 'Ne Sit Ancillae Tibi Amor Pudori' which translates as 'Don't be Ashamed of your Love for a Maid'. It ends:

Oh, graceful housemaid, full and fair,
I love your shy, imperial air,
And always loiter on the stair
When you are going by.
A strict reserve, the fates demand;
But, when to let you pass I stand,
Sometimes by chance I touch your hand
And sometimes catch your eye.

Stevenson called Hyères, 'that sweet corner of the universe. The most wonderful view into a moonlit garden. Angels, I know, frequent it and it thrills all night to the flutes of silence'. There he wrote more than half of a novel about a prostitute, *The Travelling Companion*, and declared himself pleased with it. Fanny wasn't, though, and it ended up being burned after a sharp exchange. She was his self-appointed agent and literary advisor. 'I am now as she has made me,' he said resignedly. As he wrote to Henley:

I sleep upon my art for a pillow; I waken in my art; I am unready for death because I hate to leave it. I love my wife, I do not know how much, nor can, nor shall, unless I lose her; but while I can conceive of my being widowed, I refuse the offering of life without my art...

Fanny always thought she knew best on every practical matter, if only because she had been allowed to do so for too long. Stevenson was hemmed in by Osbournes.

In January 1884 Henley and Baxter, like a blustering cavalry, came to the rescue. Henley's boisterous laughter and Baxter's calm assurance did much to restore Stevenson to something of his old self. They were an unlikely pairing, the west-country wordsmith and the Edinburgh solicitor, but they were bonded in their regard for each other and for their sick friend. Ignoring Fanny's protests, they swept him off to Nice with them. Unfortunately, after three days of celebratory drinking, he collapsed with a haemorrhage on the Promenade des Anglais. Sheepishly, they sent for a doctor. Though Henley wanted to stay, Fanny was adamant they should leave.

As soon as Baxter and Henley had gone, however, Stevenson's condition deteriorated and Fanny panicked. Doctors were called in one after another, to the utter confusion of everyone. An infection set in, followed by delirium. Thinking this was the end, Fanny cabled Colvin to come at once – she needed a man to make the funeral arrangements. But Colvin was not free. She cabled Simpson in Edinburgh, but he didn't even reply. She had cried 'wolf' about Louis too often. Eventually, the 'other Stevenson half', Bob, came to help and Louis was gingerly brought back to Hyères, a virtual cadaver. It had been a close call – Louis said he could hear 'the creak of Charon's rowlocks'.

Louis gradually began to rally again and Bob went back to England. He was an impatient invalid. 'The doctor told me to leave off wine, to regard myself as an old man and to sit by my fire. None of which I wish to do.'

Then, tested like Job, he was struck down by opthalmia and lay blindfolded in bed, his right hand strapped to his side, blood spurting from his mouth in a repeat of previous haemorrhages. Writing on a slate held up by Fanny he scrawled, 'If this is death, it's an easy one.' Fanny was utterly distraught. She sent to England for a Dr Mennell who recommended complete rest and inertia: no talking and no writing. This austere regimen was exquisite torture for Stevenson, but he persevered. He had no alternative.

His recovery once more underway, Fanny did what she did best – she moved house again. Their French exile had seen them domiciled at Hyères, Lyon, Vichy, Clermont Ferrand and finally at the

Hôtel Chabassière at Royat. When finally the 'blind, blood-spitting, somnolent, superannuated son of a bedpost, rotten-ripe' left his much-loved France, it was never to see it again.

He was never to forget one particular house in France: La Solitude, rue de la Pierre Glissante, Hyères-les-Palmiers. 'I was only really happy once' he said years later, 'and that was at Hyères.'

No woman should marry a teetotaller
or a man who does not smoke.
VIRGINIBUS PUERISQUE

CHAPTER NINE

A Shilling Shocker

So long as we love, we serve,
so long as we are loved by others,
I would say we were indispensable.
LAY MORALS

FANNY HAD BEEN told by one of the many doctors consulted in France, 'Keep him alive till forty, and then, though a winged bird, he may live to ninety.' Crusty old Dr Drummond had said that Louis could live till he was seventy, if only he would stop 'this damned travelling about'. As if it were all Stevenson's idea. He had always had the urge to travel, but the business of moving from house to house was largely driven by his wife.

At thirty-seven he had no wish to be a 'sit-by-the-fire', but his poor health dictated that he had to watch his step. He was aware that he had survived 'where many a stronger man might not...'

There had been a moment in the hectic French emergency when Fanny (at forty-four) had thought she might be pregnant; when that possibility passed, Stevenson had declared himself to be *inconsolable*. But that, too, passed.

News came from Henley about that other Stevenson child, the play, *Deacon Brodie*. While Louis was still in France it had opened, on 21 December 1882, at Pullen's Theatre of Varieties in Bradford. It was 'hissed off the stage'. The Haldane Crichton Company, undaunted, went on to tour the north of England billing it as 'The New Scotch National Drama', although the lead was played an Englishman, Edward Henley, William's younger brother. This young man was to become something of a thorn in Stevenson's flesh.

The Edinburgh *Courant* reported on 2 January 1883:

> The appearance of Mr Robert Louis Stevenson as a dramatist cannot fail to be interesting to the admirers of that pleasing and very original writer. His play, written in collaboration with Mr W.E. Henley... bears the title *Deacon Brodie, or, The Double Life* and is founded on a well-known Edinburgh tradition...

Another critic considered that:

> As a joint production by two young writers... one of whom has already established himself as one of the first humorists and most picturesque essayists of the day, *Deacon Brodie* has strong claims upon our attention...

This notice proved two things: Stevenson was already a name and people wanted the play to succeed. The possibility of theatrical success reawakened Henley's enthusiasm for the drama and reopened the whole question of playwriting for Stevenson. He had seen *The Pirates of Penzance* in San Francisco in 1880 (incidentally, this turned out to be his last visit to a theatre) and had hardly given a thought to things theatrical since then. Now here was Henley suggesting reworking *Deacon Brodie* yet again. Stevenson replied, 'The *Deacon* can't be tackled until my health and my head are reinstated.' However, once he was installed in lodgings at Richmond-on-Thames, it was one of the first projects he took up, though 'the coffers were low again' and he wondered if he could afford the time. Henley had gained the promise of a production of *Brodie*; his brother Edward was prepared to invest an unexpected legacy of one hundred pounds on staging a matinée performance at Mr Gooch's Theatre, Leicester Square.

Even Fanny was caught up in the excitement of the enterprise. In 1881 she had added a candid postscript to one of Stevenson's letters to Henley:

Do keep your eagle eye upon the stage where I am convinced a gold mine shows out. Something that you and I and Louis may work to our great advantage. A gold mine is very necessary to us all and you'll find it nowhere else. With brim purses, think what we could do. And the freedom that a little money gives, think what it would do for your wife, to say nothing of Louis's wife who is greedy for gold.

Everyone who was anyone in London arts and letters attended the matinée on 2 July 1884 – with the notable exception of Stevenson himself. He wasn't well enough to leave his bed. It was probably just as well. The audience was put off by the Scottish dialect and press reaction was lukewarm, although not completely discouraging – 'With all its shortcomings, *Deacon Brodie* is a play that contains distinct promise of better things to come.' Margaret Stevenson's opinion is not recorded, nor is Fanny's.

The Savile circle generally loathed it, some taking the view that playwriting was not a proper pursuit for a gentleman of letters. Henry James, a genuine theatre-lover, made no comment – and that was comment enough. Henley, ever the optimist, thought they could develop it further, but he generously conceded, '... the match is no longer equal. Louis has grown faster than I have'. Stevenson's general perspective was that, 'Work done, for the artist, is the Golden Goose killed; you sell its feathers and lament the eggs. Tomorrow, the fresh woods.' Elsewhere he said, 'the *Deacon* is damned bad'. *Deacon Brodie* was not ready to lie down. While Edward Henley took the play to America, Stevenson went back to his books and finished off *More New Arabian Nights*, which he had begun at Hyères.

'The old Hawes Inn made a call upon my fancy. A boat fraught with a dear cargo put off from the Queen's Ferry...' This thought was to lead to *Kidnapped*, which was begun at Bournemouth eary in 1885, 'partly as a lark and partly as a pot-boiler' for James Henderson of *Young Folks* but not finished until the spring of the following year due to Stevenson's feeling 'entirely worked out'. This didn't stop him adding a sequel, *The Adventures of David Balfour*, which came out later in a two-volume edition of *Kidnapped* published by Cassell and Company after his death. So it would seem that the Bournemouth Stevenson wasn't entirely worked out after all.

Bournemouth was to be the last place in England where Stevenson would live for any significant time. Fanny favoured the move: Lloyd was at school there and the sea-air was potentially health-giving. In early summer 1884 they moved into 'Wensleydale', a house set on the cliffs with views over to the Isle of Wight. Stevenson resumed his collaboration with Henley, hoping that lessons had been learned and that this time they would write a play that sparkled like their talk. Lloyd Osbourne recalled Henley's invasion:

> Henley came – a great, glowing, massive-shouldered fellow with a big, red beard and a crutch; jovial, astoundingly clever, and with a laugh that rolled out like music... and he had come to make us all rich!... RLS was no longer to plod along as he'd been doing; Henley was to abandon his ill-paid editorships; they would write plays that would run for a hundred nights and make them thousands of pounds...

Perhaps he ought to have said 'one hundred and one nights', for it was that much of dream. Nevertheless, *Beau Austin,* a comedy, was written – in four days. *Admiral Guinea* was written virtually in tandem, and with the same drink-fuelled zest. With both plays complete and the whisky decanter empty, Henley took himself back to Edinburgh.

Fanny's dead hand can be seen on Stevenson's next project, *The Dynamiters*. However, that 'lovely autumn', she at least contrived a positive household move to Bonallie Towers, among the pines of Branksome Park, Stevenson's 'three Bs' – 'Bonallie Towers, Branksome Park, Bournemouth'. The one thing Bonallie Towers did not have was a tower, but the situation was good and one could smell the sea as well as the pines. Just what the doctors had ordered.

As soon as they had settled in, visitors started to arrive. Bob Stevenson, much to Fanny's delight, followed by the irrepressible

Henley, much to her annoyance, with a heavy cold. Valentine Roch became adept at smoothing over the awkwardness between 'The Bedlamite' and 'Buffalo William'. Fanny did make some effort to establish friendly relations with Henley, but even these were barbed. For instance, she had written to him: 'You know we love you in spite of your many faults, so try to bear with our few.' (Henley's response had been dismissive: 'I think, Mrs Lewis, that we'd better give up corresponding on any save the commonest subjects.') Lloyd, on the other hand, was swept off his feet by Henley's 'unimaginable fire and vitality' and regarded the editor as someone who might assist his entry into the world of letters. But Lloyd could not stick at anything for long.

Tom Stevenson's wedding present to Louis and Fanny – a house, complete with five hundred pounds to cover furnishings and fittings, may be seen as an attempt to keep his son in Britain. The anchor had been thrown over the side of the matrimonial barque and Stevenson could hear the chains rattling as the iron bit on the sea-bed of his family loyalties. The carefree Bohemian was temporarily snared by home comforts and the pleasing prospect of having no more rent to pay. They moved into 61 Alum Chine that Easter. The first thing Stevenson did was order a cellar of good wine. Fanny had to return briefly to Hyères and in her absence Valentine slept in Stevenson's room – on a couch by the fire.

Stevenson named the house Skerryvore, after one of his father's lighthouses, and placed a model lighthouse at the door, with the legend, 'I, on the lintel of this cot, inscribe the name of a strong tower'.

> I was dwindling into a burgher – or is it burgess? I never know which. Whatever it is, I hate the word. And I was slightly uneasy with the thought that over our heads was our very own roof-tree... I lent myself to be converted into a householder... Fanny is a born home-maker – everything large of their kind – and soon we had a blue room, a miniature

stables... and the whole place a veritable labyrinth of paths, bowers, arbours and escape rooms. When the vicar called it took him hours to find us...

Neighbours included Sir Percy Shelley, the poet's elderly son, who was convinced that Stevenson was his father's reincarnation. Sir William and Lady Taylor and their daughter Una became good friends. Other visitors included William Archer, a Scottish drama critic, and John Singer Sargent, whose perceptive portrait of RLS shows him wafting across the canvas like a whiff of cigarette-smoke.

In August 1885 Stevenson and Fanny paid a visit to Thomas Hardy in nearby Dorchester. Fanny took an immediate dislike to the eminent author's wife, Emma, commenting with unintended personal resonance, 'What very strange marriages literary men seem to make.' The two men got on well enough and when, some time later, Stevenson asked if he might dramatise *The Mayor of Casterbridge*, Hardy was delighted – 'I feel several inches taller at the idea...' However, the project was never taken forward and Hardy felt insulted. Stevenson began to share Henry James's distaste for the man.

At least he and Fanny could agree on Henry James. She saw him as an ally – not least because of his dislike of Henley – and said his frequent visits saved her sanity. Hurricane Henley had practically destroyed it during the summer, when he had been a daily visitor. Sir Herbert Beerbohm Tree, the actor-manager of the Haymarket Theatre in London, had shown interest in presenting *Beau Austin* – but only, 'sometime in the future'. He suggested that they rewrite the melodrama, *Robert Macaire*, based on the original French success of the same name. Stevenson called their finished script, 'a piece of job-work, hurriedly bockled'. After a further unsatisfactory collaboration, this time with Fanny, on *The Hanging Judge*, he finally brought down the curtain on drama projects. Henley limped back to Grub Street, still convinced that their plays *ought* to have worked. But they were just too polished, and lacked the rough edge of reality that makes stage dialogue work. As collaborators, Stevenson and Henley tended to cancel each other out. Having said that, it is interesting to note how well so many of Stevenson's novels lend themselves to adaptation for the screen. In more ways than one, he was a man ahead of his time.

The essential theme of *Deacon Brodie* would soon be triumphantly realised in the novel that would bring him international fame: *The Strange Case of Dr Jekyll and Mr Hyde*. Longmans had suggested 'a shilling shocker' for the Christmas trade and for two days Stevenson 'went about racking [his] brain for any kind of plot'. In 'A Chapter on Dreams', he recounts that he had been trying to find 'a body, a vehicle for that strong sense of man's double being'. His recent dramatic preoccupations inspired a dream of 'a man being pressed into a cabinet, when he swallowed a drug and changed into another being'. Stevenson awoke knowing that he had found the missing link. Everything fell into place, 'and before [he] again went to sleep almost every detail of the story was clear'. It is worth recalling here that the cabinet in his bedroom at Heriot Row had been made by that notorious Master Carpenter, William Brodie. However, the *play* based on Brodie, rather the actual history of the man, provides the true provenance of *Dr Jekyll and Mr Hyde*. Working on the stage character of Brodie had intensified Stevenson's fascination with duality. Through his own direct experience of medicinal cocaine and laudanum, he knew what it was to cross the boundary between the real and the hallucinatory – provoking the fascinating question: How hallucinatory is reality, and how real is hallucination? Stevenson would also have been aware of Dr James Simpson's experiments with chloroform – indeed, with his friend Walter, Simpson's son, he had been in the very room where they were conducted.

The first draft was written in a white heat over three days – 'I drive on with Jekyll; bankruptcy at my heels'. It was thrown into the fire, after Fanny said she didn't like it. The next morning Stevenson embarked on a second draft, 'from another point of view'. In three more days, after revisions, the brilliant allegory was finished. As he wrote to FWH Myers, '*Jekyll* was conceived, written, rewritten, re-re-written and printed, inside ten weeks.' It sold over 40,000 copies in the first six months of 1886. The book's success was sealed when a sermon was preached in St Paul's denouncing it. It was a sensation and certainly a far greater work than the 'shilling shocker' he was originally commissioned to produce. To achieve this masterpiece, Stevenson put his own contradictions under the aesthetic microscope and in creating the monster out of himself, he at last spat out the devil of hypocrisy that had been tormenting him since adolescence. The novel marks the maturing of Robert Louis Stevenson.

Around noon on 8 May 1887, Tom Stevenson fell asleep in his chair in the drawing-room at Heriot Row, never to wake up again. Louis and Fanny had been summoned by telegram the day before and had seen him just before the end. It was a terrible sight: the strong, stern father now 'a changeling', sitting there in broadcloth and cravat, smoking his pipe, staring straight ahead, recognising no one but the approaching angel. He died with his best boots on (just as his son would).

According to Stevenson, his father had seen life 'as a shambling sort of omnibus taking him to his hotel'. He had now arrived at the terminus, and was glad to get off. He was buried in the New Calton Cemetery but Stevenson was unable to attend – he had jaundice, and was coughing up blood, and as his uncle George pointed out, there was 'only room in the coffin for one'.

Stevenson's condition deteriorated and he was urgently advised to leave Britain. By this time, *Jekyll and Hyde,* his 'bogie tale', was taking the United States by storm and he was eager to go there and taste his new celebrity. Fanny was not quite so keen: 'Louis is wild to start for America at once, which seems madness to me.' For the first time in their marriage, Stevenson asserted himself. Physically weak as he was, he was now his own man, never to be at her total behest again. He had lived long enough 'like a weevil in a biscuit'. He pulled his hand out of the Vandegrift 'steam press' and pointed his finger west. They *would* go to America, and that was that.

Margaret Stevenson surprised them all by announcing that she was going with them, adding that henceforth she preferred to be addressed as 'Aunt Maggie'. A new order was emerging. Fanny was about to discover the steel beneath the Balfour velvet. She was persuaded to put Skerryvore up for sale. She was brokenhearted but her husband was relieved to see it go:

> I was virtually a prisoner in the place for as long as I lived in it. I could not step on the lawn without permission. But the drawing room, the yellow room was beautiful. It was like eating just to sit in it. I blush for the figure I cut in such a bower. I left my youth in Bournemouth. Not that I minded. I was lucky to have had it for so long.

> *To be truly happy is a question of how we*
> *begin and not of how we end,*
> *of what we want and not of what we have.*
> EL DORADO

CHAPTER TEN

Divided Loyalties

Life is a permanent possibility of sensation.
AES TRIPLEX

ALMOST AS SOON AS HE was out in the Atlantic on the *Ludgate Hill*, Stevenson's whole being seemed to surge with a sense of release. With three thousand pounds in the bank and more to come once the lawyers had sorted out his father's estate, he could do what he liked and go where he wanted:

I was so happy on board that ship, I could not have believed it possible... I had literally forgotten what happiness was, and the full mind – full of external and physical things, not of cares and labours... my heart literally sang.

Henry James had sent a case of champagne as a 'going-away' gift. 'They are a romantic lot – and I delight in them,' he said. Stevenson and his mother, both excellent sailors, finished most of it between them, offering it to the others as a seasickness remedy.

At New York the press had turned out in force to meet the famous author of *Dr Jekyll and Mr Hyde*. After two days of interviews and photographs at the Victoria Hotel, Stevenson fled to stay with friends in Rhode Island. ('What a silly thing is popularity,' he said.) Around this time, the American sculptor Augustus Saint-Gaudens created a medallion showing him in typical pose, propped up in bed balancing a book or piece of writing on his knees.

Lucrative propositions flooded in. *New York World* offered him ten thousand dollars a year for a weekly column, while *Scribner's* was prepared to pay three thousand dollars apiece for twelve monthly articles. While he pondered his options, Fanny went ahead with Lloyd into the Adirondacks in search of a place to rent near Saranac, where Dr Edward Trudeau, himself a consumptive, ran a clinic for fellow-sufferers. She found some rather basic accommodation above Saranac Lake. There was an element of roughing it but they all settled in quickly and Stevenson got back into his routine, writing in the morning and walking in the afternoon.

Fanny again felt unwell and left for New York, 'to see proper doctors', and to take Lloyd to Boston for a third try at tertiary education. In her absence, Margaret Stevenson managed everything. She was full of energy; the sombre shadow of her husband had lifted, and the gutsy girl who had always been there was revealed. She and Fanny, in their different ways, were bossy women, the difference being that everyone liked Maggie, and would do anything for her. Her determination was cloaked in diffidence; as Will Low commented, 'one of her most charming traits was the modest assumption of surprise that she should be the mother of so brilliant a son'.

Fanny returned to Saranac briefly, then she was off again to make family visits. Hardly back from that trip, she departed for Montreal, 'to buy winter clothing for everyone'. They now had money and she was making sure it was spent – and also that she would spend as little time as possible in the mountains. She visited New York again, then, in March 1888, made the long trip to California to see her family. Belle and her seven-year-old grandson, Austin met her there. The Strongs were still based in Hawaii, still receiving money from Stevenson and forever asking for more. Stevenson's generosity of spirit was remarkable. He wrote to Fanny:

My dearest Fellow,
Doubts as to your movements have withheld me from really writing, and I do not know if you will get this... As for us we get on thoroughly well, Valentine and my Mother go along most pleasantly; I do hope all is well in that quarter... Lloyd is really going ahead... after a fashion... I have sent B. forty dollars in the meanwhile...

Fanny's restlessness hardly made for marital bliss. In December Stevenson told a correspondent, 'My wife is no great shakes; the place does not suit her – it is my private opinion that no place does...' He took a small revenge by ordering everything he could think of to be sent up from the New York shops, including 'a baccy-box with [his] name on it'. One thing he could not procure at any price was conventional wifely duty. But then, he was not a conventional man. Whenever Fanny imagined she was ill, she took off. When she was about the house, she was a domestic tyrant. The constant disruption perhaps explains the mediocrity of much of Stevenson's work around this time – a reworking of *The Hanging Judge*, *The Wrong Box* (co-written with Lloyd), and *The Black Arrow*. His 'A Memoir of Fleeming Jenkin' published in *Nature* magazine in London was a more typically resonant piece. He turned down the chance of writing a full biography of his own father for an Edinburgh publisher, although he did jot down bits and pieces from time to time, sketches, no more, as if he was afraid of tackling the full portrait. In the margin of one essay, 'Thomas Stevenson: Civil Engineer', opposite his father's view that 'any woman should have a divorce for the asking', he had written 'Any man or woman who wants a divorce should have it for registering his or her wish...'

Over Christmas and into the New Year of 1888 his household was snowbound, but so Scottish did it all seem that Stevenson loved it, despite his frostbitten ears, a minor complaint after all he'd been through. So far, not a drop of red blood stained the virgin snows. Stevenson gleefully braved temperatures well below zero, wrapped up in his Montreal furs and with three pairs of gloves on. *The Master of Ballantrae* was begun – yet another working of the duality theme, this time between two brothers. In a passage that may have reflected his mood at time of writing, Mackeller, the steward, says:

I never had much tolerance for the female sex. My own mother was certainly one of the salt of the earth, and my Aunt Dixon, who paid my fees at University [was] a very notable woman... but as for the female sex, being far from a bold man, I have ever shunned their company. Not only do I see no cause to regret this diffidence in myself, but have invariably remarked that most unhappy consequences follow those who were less wise.

The character of Mackellar, ambiguous and multilayered, has his genesis in Jekyll.

It is a strange art... to talk for hours of a thing, and never name nor yet so much as hint at it. And I remember I wondered if it was by some such natural skill that the Master made love to Mrs Henry all day long (as he manifestly did) without startling her into reserve.

Shades of the tacit Stevenson-Valentine relationship, perhaps?

The winter sped by with Stevenson deeply engrossed in *The Master*, ultimately one of his finest efforts. But there was a serpent in his frosty Eden. Fanny worked on him until she had persuaded him that he needed a change. Her addiction to upheaval, her efforts to involve the lesser literary talents of herself and her son in his writing projects, her encouragement of her daughter's parasitic attitude, the chronic stress she created – all this amounted to the slow killing of RLS. Her protestations that all her actions were for his benefit do not stand up to examination, whatever her conscious intentions.

At this point, Henley launched the opening salvo in the infamous 'Nixie' quarrel which was to part the two old friends for good. Reading *Scribner's Magazine* in March 1887, he was astonished to come across a story entitled 'Nixie', with the author given as Fanny Vandegrift Stevenson. He wrote immediately to Stevenson: 'It's Katharine's; surely, it's Katharine's? There are even reminiscences of phrases and imagery, parallel incidents.... why there wasn't a double signature is what I've not been able to understand...' The background to this is that the previous year the Stevensons had been at the Henleys in Shepherd's Bush; Katharine De Mattos (Louis's cousin and Bob Stevenson's sister) had told the company a story she was writing about a girl who escapes from an asylum and meets a young man on a train. Fanny, in her intrusive, tactless way, suggested that the story would be improved if the girl were instead, a 'nixie', or water sprite, and offered to collaborate with Katharine on it. Katharine politely demurred. Fanny then asked if she could rewrite it in her way, and when Katharine, again politely, hesitated, she took it that no answer meant a 'yes' and proceeded to rewrite the story as soon as she was back in the United States. One of Fanny's reasons for visiting New York had been to sell her reworking of Katharine's story to *Scribner's*.

Was Stevenson consulted? Surely, if he had read it, he would have pointed out the plagiarism? Henley was incandescent. To his mind, Katherine not only deserved a credit but also a share of the fee, particularly considering she was in tight financial circumstances following her recent divorce.

Guilty as he might have felt, Stevenson chivalrously took his wife's part against Henley, just as Henley played the knight-errant for Katharine. Their old, dear, tested and tried friendship suffered irreparably. This heart-breaking development gave Henley further reason to detest that 'neurotic, semi-educated woman' whose 'presumption and arrogance' had come between them. He could never get over Fanny's conceit in thinking that she could write as well as her husband.

In 1901, seven years after Stevenson's death, Henley wrote a touching memoir of his old friend for *Pall Mall Magazine*:

> I take a view of Stevenson that is my own and decline to be concerned with this seraph in chocolate, this barley-sugar effigy of a real man... the best and most interesting part of Stevenson's life will never be written – even by me.

Posterity can only regret this. Henley thought he should have been

Stevenson's biographer. Fanny saw to it that he was not. This may have added an element of pique to his review of Graham Balfour's official *Life*:

> the Stevenson he knew was not the Stevenson who came to me... I remember rather, the unmarried Lewis, the friend, the comrade, the *charmeur*. Truly, that last word, French as it is, is the only one worthy of him. I shall ever remember him as that. The impression of his writing disappears; the impression of himself and of his talk is ever a possession. He had... all the gifts (he and his cousin Bob) that qualify the talker's temperament – voice and eye and laugh, look and gesture, humour and fantasy, audacity and agility of mind, a lively and most impudent invention, a copious vocabulary, a right gift for foolery, a just, inevitable sense of right and wrong... Those who know him by his books – (and I think our Fleeming Jenkin, were he alive, would back me here) know but the poorest of him. Forasmuch as he was primarily a talker, his printed works... are but a sop for posterity.

In spring 1888, Stevenson led his entourage out of their icebound cave on the hill, back to New York and a comfortable hotel. One of the first things they heard there was that Edward Henley had caused the American tour of *Deacon Brodie* to be abandoned because of his drunken, riotous behaviour in Philadelphia, and that he was staying in expensive hotels and directing the charges to Stevenson, who exploded at his effrontery:

> I have long groaned under this slavery to Teddy, a young man in whom I do not believe, and whom I much dislike... and the drunken, whoreson bugger and bully living himself in the best hotels and smashing inoffensive strangers in the bar! It is all too sickening.

After the previous winter's high, Stevenson was as low in spirits as he had been for years. *The Master of Ballantrae* was stuck at Chapter Six. Will Low arranged for the party to be lodged in the little colonial inn at Manasquan, across the Hudson River in New Jersey, a pleasant spot where Stevenson could relax and indulge his love of being on the water, and with great zest he took up cat-boat sailing.

Meanwhile, Fanny was dispatched to San Francisco with a banker's order for two thousand pounds and instructions to find a vessel and crew to take all of them into the Pacific. The idea was that Stevenson would write up a journal and Lloyd would take photographs which could be used as illustrations for the resulting series of articles and book, which would fund the adventure. The plan seemed to please everyone. Stevenson dreamed of seeing Japan at last, then returning to Britain by way of Fiji, Tonga, Ceylon and Marseilles. As Lloyd recalled, he planned to:

> walk into the Savile Club and electrify his old friends as the returned seafarer from the South Seas Islands. At least, he was constantly dwelling on this phase of his return and choosing the exact hour when he would make the most dramatic entrance.

He little realised that there would be no such return from his odyssey into South Seas. But he must have had in mind the words of Mark Twain, spoken on a chance encounter in Washington Square: the great American author had recommended New Zealand as being perfect for his health – echoing what Charles Stoddard had said, and William Seed's visit to Heriot Row all those years before, with his stories of Samoa.

The fateful cable arrived:

> Can secure splendid, sea-going schooner-yacht *Casco* for seven hundred and fifty pounds monthly with most comfortable accommodation for six aft and six forward. Can be ready for sea in ten days. Reply immediately...

Stevenson replied while the telegraph messenger waited, 'Blessed girl, take the yacht and expect us in ten days.' The die was cast. The old excitement was rising. In his letters, one can feel it in behind every word. He couldn't wait to tell everyone. On 28 May he wrote to Henry James from Manasquan:

> This, dear James, is a valedictory. On June 15th, the schooner yacht, *Casco*, will (weather and jealous Providence permitting) steam through the Golden Gates for Honolulu, Tahiti, the Galapagos, and – I hope – not the bottom of the Pacific. It will contain your obedient 'umble servant and party. It seems too good to be true and is a very good way of getting through the green-sickness of maturity, which, with all its accompanying ills, is now declaring itself in my mind and life... In three days I leave for San Francisco.

The 'Nixie' quarrel with Henley had drained him. He could not rid his mind of the 'affair', as he called it, and every time he thought about it he felt ill. It would take something big to blow it out of his head. Well, as he was soon to find out, the Pacific was big. On the last day of May, with his mother, Lloyd and Valentine, he crossed the Hudson again to catch the Chicago train from New York. Maggie had chipped in a thousand pounds of her own money towards expenses, and they travelled first class whenever possible. However, an eight hour wait in Chicago before boarding the rail-car to Salt Lake City did nothing to improve Stevenson's opinion of the American railroad car. He wrote to a correspondent:

> I myself dread, worse than almost any other imaginable peril, the miraculous and really insane invention, the American railroad car. Heaven help the man – may I add the woman – that sets foot in one. Ah, if it were only an ocean to cross, it would be a matter of small thought to me – and great pleasure. But the railroad car – every man has his weak point; and I

fear the railroad car as abjectly as I do an earwig, and, on the whole on better grounds.

Coming from the former 'amateur emigrant' this is perhaps understandable, but now he was a man of means. Getting to San Francisco meant a long haul over the High Sierras to meet Fanny in Sacramento on 7 June. She was wearing a new hat. (It actually belonged to Belle, who had come to San Francisco to wave them off.) Fanny hinted at marriage difficulties between Belle and Joe, but Stevenson was too tired to think about anything other than the bath and bed waiting for him at the Occidental Hotel, situated on the Bay with views out to the beckoning Pacific.

There is no record of how Belle reacted on seeing 'Lulu' again after seven years, or of his response to her. She was an attractive woman, for all her matrimonial difficulties. Not that there was time for such considerations. There were other, more important matters to settle, such as confirmation of the hire of the vessel. This was not as certain as Stevenson had thought. Dr Merritt, the owner of the *Casco*, loved it like a baby and was very fussy about who should sail in it. He insisted on an interview with the Stevensons before confirming arrangements. Luckily, the author was on top form and they got the ship for five hundred monthly, with liability for repairs. Captain Otis was none too sure of Stevenson at first, but he was won round, just as Dr Merritt had been. Stevenson had the gift of making people like him – that is, if he liked them. Otis invited Stevenson to see over the *Casco* at Oakland Creek. Originally designed as a topsail racing schooner, the vessel was in wonderful condition, the decks white and the brasswork gleaming. Stevenson worked out possible routes with Otis. This was *Treasure Island* for real, and he was like a little boy in anticipation of the adventure, more so than Lloyd, who followed all the talk over the maps, wide-eyed but uncomprehending. It really mattered little to him where he went, as long as it wasn't a school or college. He was already living a life which, it must be said, had all the usefulness of minor royalty.

Fanny lost herself in a pre-voyage shopping spree, never letting Belle stray far from her side. No doubt she would have preferred Belle to have been coming, rather than Valentine. On Belle's advice the three sea-going ladies were fitted by a Chinese tailor with *holakus*, or 'Mother Hubbards', long, loose-fitting robes in muslin or lawn which precluded the need for corsets. Aunt Maggie said the outfits made them look 'queer-looking customers'; she most certainly was, since she insisted on also wearing her white widow's cap.

When they all went aboard, the celebrations started almost at once. The tugboat *Pelican* went busily back and forward to the *Casco* as it lay off Telegraph Hill, bringing friends and flowers and a whole herd of press and photographers. Drink flowed and everybody talked at once. Despite all this the social jollity Stevenson betrayed a rather more sombre mood in a letter to Charles Baxter:

> O, I go on my journey with a bitter heart. It will be best for all I dare say, if the *Casco* goes down with me. For there's devilish little left to live for.

They were delayed until dawn on Thursday the 28th. Dora Williams pressed a farewell message into Fanny's hand – '*Ave atque Vale*!' ('Hail and Farewell'). It was off with the old and on with the new. Stevenson's sense of foreboding lifted with the anchor – perhaps prematurely: even before they had cleared the Golden Gate, Valentine Roch had injured herself falling down a hatchway.

By this time Fanny was already 'dying' in her bunk. Lloyd thought seasickness was contagious and kept to his cabin. Aunt Maggie, however, helped herself to what was left of the champagne, while Stevenson stood at the bow, smoking. As the Scottish author Compton Mackenzie once whimsically observed, not since the owl and the pussy-cat put to sea in their pea-green boat or the men of Gothan in their tub, had a more eccentric set of passengers set off in a vessel. Captain Otis must have wondered what he had let himself in for.

As the *Casco* pointed on a south-west course to the Marquesas

Islands, five thousand sea miles away, the figure of Belle could be seen on the wharf, waving her scarf to the last.

*An aim in life is the only fortune worth
the finding; and it is not to be found in foreign
lands but in the heart itself.*

THE AMATEUR EMIGRANT

CHAPTER ELEVEN

Such Beautiful Scenes

Old and young, we are all on our last cruise.
If there's a fill of tobacco among the crew,
for God's sake pass it round, and let
us have a pipe before we go.
CRABBED AGE AND YOUTH

JUST BEFORE LEAVING, Stevenson had written to Colvin:

> I have no more hope in anything than a dead frog. I go into
> everything with a composed despair, and don't mind – just as I
> always go to sea with the conviction that I am to be drowned,
> and [yet] I like it before all other pleasures.

Perhaps that was just the Scot in him – expect the worst and you'll
never be disappointed. Or was he merely being realistic? Stevenson's
gamble in going over this unpredictable ocean in a ninety-five-foot
racing yacht of a mere seventy-two tons register with a reluctant
captain and a minimal crew was either courageous or foolhardy
– or very Stevensonian.

> The truth is, I was far through (if you understand Scots) and
> came none too soon to the South Seas, where I was to recover
> peace of body and mind...

Captain Otis made his way by dead reckoning towards their
first landfall in the Marquesas Islands. Complete with typewriter,
camera and magic lantern, they were about to explore Polynesia.
Their cabin luggage was loaded with all the paraphernalia of the

camera age: plate glass, development paper, tripods and a Kodak camera with collapsible bellows.

While the *Casco* raced south-west, all, apart from Fanny, were 'pretty gay on board' and spent their time 'photographing, draught-playing and skylarking like anything'. However, a freak squall just before they reached the Marquesas caused a cascade of salt water to flood into some of the cabins. After that, they made sure the portholes were kept closed. Three weeks out of San Francisco, the lookout sighted land. In fact, three islands hove in sight through the shimmering heat – Ua-huna on the port bow, Ua-pu to the south and abeam, Nuka-hiva. The *Casco* was soon lying at her moorings in Anaho Bay. Stevenson was elated:

> This, at last, is my beau-ideal! The climate is simply perfect... everything is looking new-made and beautiful... we all feel we want to 'draw in our chairs' and stay here a considerable time... At last I have an open-air life...

While half-naked Polynesians clambered aboard from canoes to explore every inch of the ship, Aunt Maggie studiously carried on with her reading, quite unperturbed. She spent a lot of time reading. (She also tried to get Captain Otis to read her son's books in the ship's library, but he had stubbornly refused to oblige – he said he had read *Treasure Island*, and that was enough. His candour greatly amused Stevenson.)

In the weeks the *Casco* lay at anchor, the party sometimes went ashore on chicken shoots. Coming back from one such excursion, Lloyd dropped his camera overboard. When a replacement was purchased on reaching Hiva-Oa, the spoiled boy expressed surprise at being expected to pay for it.

The *Casco* now moved to Tai-o-hae on the other side of the island, where Ah Fu, a Chinese cook who would be with them for some time, came aboard. As they moved through the perilous waters of the archipelago, Stevenson offered a lift to a French missionary lay-brother, Michel Blanc, who brought aboard a gift of sheep and pigs from the Catholic Mission. Unfortunately, all the animals were swept overboard during a passage so rough that even Stevenson was seasick. To everyone's relief, the *Casco* made it safely to Taahauka Bay off Hiva-Oa before coming to anchor again. Even though it was the rainy season, Stevenson went ashore. He took the chance of getting on land whenever he could, to take long, solitary strolls. It was his thinking time.

He made various excursions, including night trips accompanied by Otis and Lloyd to visit a local chief, Moipu. On one occasion Lloyd wandered off and was briefly captured by a rival tribe, before being rescued by Moipu's men. Eventually, the *Casco*, or the 'Silver Ship' as it was called by the local people ('Is that not pretty – I think of calling a book by that name...') was towed through the Bordelais Straits by a whale boat and Captain Otis set a difficult course through the next two nights for Rotoava, the port of entry for the Paumotos. Here they were made welcome by M. Donat, the acting Vice-Resident. Not for the first time in the Pacific, Stevenson's French proved invaluable.

Stevenson befriended the pastor at Fakarava. This unusual character turned out to be an ex-convict. Coming back from visiting him Stevenson was caught in a sudden thunderstorm and developed a bad cold. Fanny panicked, as she so often did, insisting that they put to sea at once for Tahiti, where Stevenson could get proper medical attention. However, Otis refused to move through the reefs again until the squall had died down.

As soon as they arrived at Papeete, the Stevensons moved into the Hôtel de France and the doctor was called. The prognosis was so pessimistic, Fanny became hysterical. Margaret Stevenson was tight-lipped. Stevenson alone seemed calm. He sent for Otis and told him what he should do, should he not survive to see the next day. Otis was deeply impressed by his quiet stoicism. Fortunately there was no further haemorrhage, and Stevenson was still there the next morning. He spent the following three weeks recovering in a garden cottage with a view of the harbour. The *Casco*, meantime, was taken round to Taravao on the windward side. When he returned aboard, and after further experience of the schooner's aerial propensities through the reef, he jokingly asked Otis if he did not realise that 'such yachting gymnastics were rather risky sports for an invalid author to indulge in?'

When he was well enough, he was taken in a Chinese wagon to the village of Tautira where, under the protection of sub-chief Ori-a-Ori (who named Stevenson 'Teritera' – 'Splendour of the Sky'), they all rested for three days while the *Casco* underwent repairs. Dry rot had been discovered in its main mast. A Papeete beachcomber, who had once been a ship's carpenter, had to be heavily persuaded to do the job. However, he continued to keep beachcomber's hours and it was over a month before the *Casco* was ready to sail again. After cruising for five months, Stevenson was eager to get to his mail at Honolulu, Hawaii, in what was then called the Sandwich Islands.

> O, how my spirit languishes
> To step ashore on the Sanguishes;
> For there my letters wait,
> There I shall know my fate.
> O, how my spirit languishes
> To step ashore on the Sanguishes!

Despite the playful tone, he urgently needed to get in touch with his publishers in order to get funds to pay for the new mast. The *Casco* finally left Tautira for Honolulu on Christmas Day to a 21-gun salute fired on an army rifle by M. Tibeau, a French gendarme.

Soon after crossing the Equator, they were suddenly becalmed for several days on end. Everyone lolled in what shade they could find, praying for wind. But when the wind eventually did pick up and they once more sped towards Hawaii, they realised that they were running out of food. Those inert, waiting days at sea had not been bargained for and they had eaten their way through the provisions, right down to the hard tack and salted beef kept for emergencies. Well, this was an emergency. Captain Otis decided 'to crowd on all the canvas the yacht could carry and push for port'. The *Casco* was a fore-and-aft schooner built for cruising, not speed, but picking up a leading wind fifty miles north of the Equator, she fairly flew through the water, and arrived off Honolulu 'before a fine breeze at a thirteen knot clip'. As they took on the pilot just beyond the lighthouse, to Fanny's shock and Stevenson's astonishment (and, no doubt, to the sailors' amusement), Belle Strong was winched aboard, legs kicking, her flimsy dress billowing out in the wind like a welcoming flag.

The Stevensons arrived in Honolulu on 24 January 1889. They moved in with Belle and Joe in Emma Street, where the couple had lodged with Caroline Bush for six years. Stevenson and Lloyd were duly presented at the court of King Kalakaua by the Prime Minister, Mr Gibson. Joe Strong was a drinking companion of the king. His Majesty's legendary capacity for drink was borne out again a few days later when he boarded the *Casco*. In the absence of food, the party made do with champagne and brandy. When the Europeans present had recovered, Henry Poor, Mrs Bush's son, gave a *luau*, or feast, in Stevenson's honour. Several Hawaiian delicacies were on the menu and Stevenson tasted baked dog for the first time.

There were two departures at this time – one expected, the other not. Captain Otis was due to return the *Casco* to San Francisco as per contract. Stevenson was genuinely sad to see the laconic mariner go. A mutual respect had built up between them; soon afterwards, he instructed his publishers to send Otis a complete set of his works.

The unexpected departure was that of Valentine Roch. Fanny had made accusations of dishonesty and there were hints about her behaviour with the *Casco*'s crew. Long, hot days at sea had their own perils. Stevenson would only say enigmatically that it was 'the usual tale of the maid aboard the yacht'. He was sorry to part with such a loyal companion. Valentine took a lift in the *Casco* to San Francisco, where she took a job as a housekeeper, and later married and had one son. She called him Louis.

The Stevenson entourage rented a cottage next to Henry Poor's house at Waikiki. They were to be there for five months. *The Master*, as Stevenson called his work-in-progress, hung heavily over his head:

like the arm of the gallows... it is a difficult thing to write, above all in Mackellarese; and I cannot yet see my way clear. If I pull this off *The Master* will be pretty good... and even if I don't... it will still have some good stuff in it.

He did pull it off, but it was not until well into May before the final sheets were on their way to Scribner's in New York and he could relax again. Sea-bathing in the green waters of Waikiki was a highly pleasurable pastime, but Stevenson hated the brash developments that were even then in evidence. He deplored the behaviour of the Europeans to the local people – condescending at best, brutal at worst. He hated to think that he might be perceived as the same kind of *haole* – the Hawaiian name for a white man.

He found solace in work, in reading, and in the musical evenings he now enjoyed with Belle at the piano and himself on flute, joined by whatever instrument a guest might have brought along. (It was said that whenever Stevenson played his flute, the mice would come out from under the furniture.) On these soirées he would also read aloud and talk animatedly, until Fanny signalled it was the end of the evening, making the excuse that her husband was tired – whereas he could have gone on all night.

One thing he did insist upon, however, was to visit the Honourable Archibald Cleghorn, a fellow-Scot who had recently lost his wife, the Princess Likelike. Their thirteen-year-old daughter, Princess Kaiulani, became a great favourite of Stevenson's. They would sit under a banyan tree or in a grass shack at the Cleghorn house at Ainahau, and 'Mr Stenson' would tell tales about Scotland. When, not long afterwards, Cleghorn took her to Scotland to be educated, she pined for her exotic island home. Her health broke down and she eventually returned to Honolulu, where she died aged twenty-three. Before she left on this fateful journey Stevenson composed a fond poem for her, which he slipped into her autograph album. He also wrote prophetically:

When she comes to my land and her father's, and the rain

beats down upon the window (as I fear it will)... she will remember her own islands, and the shadow of the mighty tree; and she will hear the peacocks screaming in the dusk and the wind blowing in the palms; and she will think of her father sitting there alone.

Margaret Stevenson had returned to Scotland with Cleghorn. Her sister Jane was ill and her husband's affairs still needed finalising. In order to avoid being questioned about her famous son, she adopted the name of 'Mrs Steven' when travelling alone. 'After all,' she would say, 'I am nothing without my son.' Witty, but so patently untrue.

After she left, Stevenson decided to go to the island of Molokai to see the leper colony there, founded by Father Damien, a Belgian priest:

The ship reached Father Damien's leper colony at sunrise. It stood bleak and harsh – a little town with wooden houses, two churches and a great cliff wall shutting off the world to the south... A great crowd, pantomime masks in human flesh. Every diseased hand was offered – I had no gloves. The butt-ends of human beings lying there almost unrecognisable, but still breathing, still thinking still remembering... After that I lived in a passion of pity for those faces melting into bestiality. Sickened with the spectacle of abhorrent suffering and touched to the heart by the lovely and effective virtues of the helpers – a few kind nuns...

He spent eight days at the Kalaupapa settlement and ended up teaching the nuns and residents in the Bishop Home for Girls to play croquet. When the time came to leave, he found he did not have the necessary permit. He might have been marooned there indefinitely, but for the intercession of Mother Marianne who explained to the authorities that their guest was a famous writer who had to get back to Honolulu to rejoin his family. Stevenson was relieved... and slightly ashamed of his haste to get off the island and leave the nuns to their work. He was to say that he was glad to have visited

Molokai, for remembering it made him thankful for every day he lived somewhere else.

Joe Strong's behaviour was causing increasing concern. He appeared to be intent on matching King Kalakaua drink for drink, and was losing that contest. He was also losing Belle, who was spending more time with her mother than with her husband. Stevenson could only look on with increasing dismay and irritation.

Belle was following in her mother's footsteps in that she, too, had married a wastrel and had lost a boy-child. Her second son, Hervey, like his namesake, had died in infancy. Joe was an alcoholic with a taste for opium and Belle was on the lookout for a new peg to hang herself on. Clearly, something had to be done. Stevenson, or more probably Fanny, then made a decision. Belle was given two tickets, for Austin and herself, on the next steamer for Sydney. Joe was to join the Stevensons on the *Equator*. Despite Belle's stormy protests and Joe's half-hearted whining, that was the matter settled. The Strongs went their separate ways for a time, a wedge having been driven emphatically between them. Stevenson referred to them as 'a mule load of struggling cormorants'. His extended family was certainly extending him – Lloyd's most recent decision was *not* to go to Cambridge. However, life went on. The second cruise was about to begin.

On 24 June 1889 the Stevensons boarded the brand-new, sixty-four ton schooner *Equator*. The *Honolulu Pacific Advertiser* announced:

> Robert Louis Stevenson and party leave today by the trading schooner, *Equator* bound for the Gilbert Islands... It is to be hoped that Mr Stevenson will not fall victim to native spears; but in his present state of bodily health, perhaps the temptation to kill him may not be very strong.

But the truth was, he was growing stronger all the time. He came into his own again once he was aboard ship with his troupe

– which did indeed sound more like a concert party, judging by Fanny's description of their luggage – 'hand-organ, magic lantern, fiddle, guitar, banjo, flageolet and a lot of song-books'. He wrote to Lady Taylor in Bournemouth, 'My good health does not cease to be wonderful to myself'. Since he had come into the South Seas he seemed to have filled out, not so much physically but in personality and maturity. He had a whole new assurance about the way he wanted to live and work. Nonetheless, he harboured the superstition, based on what the Scottish spey-wife had told him years before in Dunoon, that he would drown at sea, despite his love of it:

I cannot say why I like the sea; no man is more cynically and constantly alive to its perils; I regard it as the highest form of gambling; and yet I love the sea as much as I hate gambling.

The Captain of the *Equator*, Denny Reid, habitually wore a Highland bonnet and was wont to burst into a chirpy chorus of Loch Lomond while he turned the ship's wheel. Stevenson, his yachting cap at a jaunty angle, was simply elated to be riding his luck again.

The air had an indescribable sweetness, soft and nimble as the cheek of health. All day long the sun flamed and at night the stars came out in regiments.

The original sailing plan had been to join the *Morning Star*, a missionary ship which had a fixed course and timetable, but better terms were available on the *Equator*, a 'pigmy trader', and Stevenson could never resist a bargain. He knew that the *Equator* would ply a much longer, as yet unspecified route that would be determined along the way by the unpredictable dictates of commerce. Yet he still fondly imagined he would be back in London within the year, little realising what their arrival in Samoa six months hence would mean. 'Whit's for ye will ne'er gang by ye', as the old Scots proverb says.

Their first landfall was at Butaritari on Friday 14 July. The Gilbert Islands were under American 'protection' and most of the population were still drunkenly celebrating American Independence Day. The mood felt volatile and for the first time in the Pacific the Stevenson party went ashore armed with revolvers. Lloyd and Fanny practised shooting on the open roadway, aiming at bottles. Fanny impressed everyone with her marksmanship; the locals got the hint, and treated the Stevenson militia with respect.

Stevenson was duly introduced to King Tebureimoa. Having announced himself to be a subject of Queen Victoria, he was much amused to be taken to be her son (and to have it intimated that the king's seventeen wives were available). It took a month for the *Equator* to complete her errands around the neighbouring islands, during which time the party spent most of their time keeping out of the way of drunken Gilbert Islanders; Stevenson argued vehemently with the German trader who supplied them with liquor, despite a supposed ban.

The travellers were glad to get to sea again. After calling in at Abaiang, Marakei and Tarawa, they reached Apemama, where the first visitor on board was King Tembinok:

There is only one great personage in the Gilberts: Tembinok of Apemama... the last tyrant, the last vestige of a dead society... Not long ago he was overgrown by fat, obscured to view, a burthen to himself. Captains visiting the island advised him to walk, and though it broke the habits of a life and the traditions of his rank, he practised the remedy with benefit. His corpulence is now portable... Where there were no fashions, none to set them, few to follow them if they were set, and none to criticise, he dressed... 'to his own heart' – now he wears a woman's dress, now a naval uniform; now (and more usually) figures in a masquerade costume of his own design; trousers and a singular jacket with shirt tails...

This bizarre figure, 'the Napoleon of the Gilberts', was master of the islands of Apemama, Aranuka and Kuria. His authority was such that no ship could land without his permission, and this permission had to be paid for with whatever caught his eye on any visiting ship. The royal collection was extensive, to say the least:

Clocks, musical boxes, blue spectacles, umbrellas, knitted waistcoats, bolts of stuff, rifles, fowling pieces, medicines, European foods, sewing machines, and, what is more extraordinary, stoves... He is possessed of the seven devils of the collector... and, with no mark of emotion, scarce even of interest, stolidly piles up the price...

He collected his English vocabulary with equally passionate eclecticism, hanging on Stevenson's every word. When the time for leave-taking came, the king told Lloyd:

I very sorry you go. Miss Stlevan, he good man, woman, he good man, boy he good man, all good man. Woman he smart all the same man. My woman, he good man no very smart. I think Miss Stlevan he big chief all the same cap'n, man-o-wa'. I think Miss Stlevan he all the same rich man, same me... all go schoona. My father he go, my uncle he go, my cousins he go, Miss Stlevan he go: all go. You no see king cry before? King all the same man; feel bad, he cry. I very sorry...

It is reported that King Tembinok wept as the *Equator* set sail.

On Sunday 4 November 1889, at sea 240 miles from Apia, Stevenson wrote to his mother to tell her to expect him home by May or June. He had in mind a new book, *The South Seas*. In a letter to Colvin, he enthused:

If I can execute what is designed, there are few better books now extant on this globe, bar the epics and the big tragedies, and histories, and the choice lyric poetics and a novel or so – none. But it is not executed yet; and let not him that putteth on his armour, vaunt himself. At least, nobody has had such stuff, such wild stories, such beautiful scenes, such singular intimacies, such manners and traditions, so incredible a mixture of the beautiful and the horrible, the savage and the civilised...

This was certainly more than the 'book of the cruise' he had originally planned and it would take all the skills of his pen; but Fanny, in her wisdom, talked him out of it. It was too big a project, she insisted. And anyway, history wouldn't sell, wouldn't bankroll their ever-increasing expenses. Stevenson acquiesced and took up *The Wrecker* instead, working on the lacklustre novel with her overrated son. How much else, one wonders, did his domestic arrangements lose for the world of the 'big' Robert Louis Stevenson? One could say that he was totally Osbourned, which means to be at the service of a close and demanding circle, which kept closing in tighter around him.

Meantime, in the first days of December the *Equator* ran before the wind to Apia and the rest of his life. Ironically, he was heard to remark, 'I am minded to stay not very long in Apia.'

To travel hopefully is a better thing than to arrive...
And the true success is to labour.
EL DORADO

CHAPTER TWELVE

A Very Meaningful Relationship

Hope looks for unqualified success;
but Faith counts certainly on failure,
and takes honourable defeat to be a form of victory.
VIRGINIBUS PUERISQUE

ON THE AFTERNOON of Saturday 7 December 1889, the Stevenson party disembarked in Apia Bay. A small boat brought them into the shallows, where they were lifted out by brawny Samoans who carried them effortlessly to shore. They made their way up the white sands towards The Beach, a row of expatriates' houses, to be met by a welcoming group of Europeans. The Reverend Clarke (who was to bury Stevenson just five years later) recorded his first impressions:

I met a little group of three European strangers – two men and a woman. The latter wore a print gown, large, gold-crescent earrings, a Gilbert Islands hat of plaited straw, encircled by a wreath of small shells, a scarlet silk scarf around her neck, and a brilliant, plaid shawl across her shoulders; her bare feet were encased in white canvas shoes, and across her back was slung a guitar... The younger of her two companions was dressed in a striped pyjama suit – the undress costume of most Europeans in these seas – a slouch hat of native make, dark-blue sun spectacles, and over his shoulders, a banjo. The other man was dressed in a shabby suit of white flannels that had seen better days, a white drill yachting cap with a prominent peak, a cigarette in his mouth, and a photographic camera in his hand. Both men were bare-footed. They had, evidently, just landed from the little schooner now lying placidly at anchor, and my first thought was that, probably, they were wandering players, *en route* to New Zealand, compelled by their poverty to take the cheap conveyance of a trading vessel.

Also there to meet them was Harry J Moors, a contact of Joe Strong's. The American-born entrepreneur noted his first impressions of RLS:

A young-looking man came forward to meet me... of fair and somewhat sallow complexion and about five feet ten inches in height. He wore a slight, scraggy moustache and his hair hung down about his neck after the fashion of artists... He was not a handsome man, and yet there was something irresistibly attractive about him... keen, enquiring eyes, brown in colour, strangely bright and seemed to penetrate you like the eyes of a mesmerist... intensely nervous, highly strung, easily excited... bubbled over with delight as one enchanted... 'It's grand!' he exclaimed.

Having been introduced to Bazett Haggard, the British Land Commissioner, Harry Sewell, the American Consul and Dr Funk, the town physician, the party began to make its way to Moors' house. On the way, they saw a procession of Samoan prisoners in chains, being led by German guards to the prison. The sight made RLS pause, but the moment passed as they passed. Moors put Stevenson up in his own home and arranged temporary accommodation for the others. This meant that Fanny and Lloyd went to one house, Joe and Ah Fu to another; Stevenson was just relieved to find that he still had land legs. Moors described him as 'fidgety':

Hardly had he got onto the street when he began to walk up and down in a most lively, not to say, eccentric manner. He could not stand still... in my house he walked about the room plying me with questions, darting up and down, with no continuity in conversation, darting questions... He had worn no shoes on the schooner, and it seemed to go very much against his will to put on any after his arrival in Apia. But before long I became aware of other eccentricities, and ceased to be surprised by anything he did...

Even when he and Fanny were installed in a rented cottage, Stevenson spent most of his time at the Moors' house. So much so, that Fanny had sometimes to come and fetch him back. It was noticed that he went reluctantly.

Joe Strong did not last long in Apia. When the *Equator* was ready to return to Sydney, Stevenson made sure he was on it. Although Joe was charming in his sober moments, these were getting rarer and everyone was glad to see the back of him.

Stevenson had felt good from the moment he set foot on the sands of Samoa, immediately sensing that its climate was better for him than all the pills and medicines that any doctor could prescribe. He bombarded Moors with questions about Samoan political affairs and the nature of German control on the island. The sight of the chained prisoners had affected him deeply.

In the evenings, he would sit on the Moors' verandah facing out to sea and 'entertain with anecdotes'. Talk was essential to Stevenson. Henley may have been right when he said Stevenson was a talker first, and writer second. Talking was the fuel that powered his writing engine. Subject matter was perhaps less important than style of utterance. Sentences fell from his lips, ready-formed and *right*, delivered with the relish that is the mark of the true wordsmith. The Samoans, with their traditional regard for oratory, respected his oral prose for the art form it was, and later honoured him as a *Matai* or Speaking Chief. Amidst all the excitement of discovering Samoa, he never failed to set aside time to work. Work was everything to him. As he once told Lloyd:

I am not a man of any unusual talent... I started out with very moderate abilities; my success has been due to my really remarkable industry – to developing what I had in me to the extreme limit. When a man begins to sharpen one faculty, and keeps on sharpening it with tireless perseverance, he can achieve wonders. Everybody knows it; it's commonplace; and yet how rare it is to find anybody doing it – I mean to the uttermost as I did. What genius I had was for work.

He was 'scribbling' for at least some part of every day, producing articles for an American magazine syndicate, and being well paid for it too. Ten thousand dollars for fifty weekly letters was a meaningful contract. He was living every writer's dream, but something made him feel guilty about it – not so much the Scottish Protestant ethic rebuking him that the sweat of the mind did not quite equate with the sweat of the brow (although sweating of any kind was easy to do in Apia). No, it was that he felt he was being overpaid for inferior work. After several half-hearted efforts (later to be expanded into *In the South Seas*), he wrote to Colvin, 'How do journalists drag up their drivel?' He explained to his publisher that he was an essayist, not a journalist, and McClure reluctantly released him from his contract, shrewdly insisting, with a view to future business, that the 'hot' author keep his advance. This made Stevenson feel even guiltier; he decided that the best thing to do with the dollars was to spend them. In this impulsive mood, he conceived the idea of building a house, although putting down roots on a tropical island was certainly not something he had planned. This enormous decision was to change his life entirely.

Perhaps another factor in his decision was that he had recently instructed Baxter to sell the family house in Heriot Row – 'Ay, ay. It is sad to sell 17; sad and fine were the old days' – but it was no more than a shell to him now, holding bitter-sweet memories. His mother would be well provided for. It was time for a change. Perhaps he felt the need to make a claim for his own bit of earth (314-and-a-half acres, to be exact). He explained to Moors:

I like this place better than any I've seen in the Pacific. Tahiti and the Marquesas pleased me. I've been to Honolulu and liked it, but this place seems more – savage.

Moors promised to find him a suitable property near Apia, on high land, and secluded enough to give him peace and quiet for his writing. 'Elbow room – it must have elbow room,' Stevenson kept saying. He had been confined to ships' cabins for too long.

In no time, Moors had found the ideal place, on the slopes of Mt Vaea, a few miles north of Apia and ten minutes' walk from the main road. It was at the junction of five streams coming from the mountain top, and for that reason was called Vailima. The two men shook hands on the deal. Stevenson was now a landowner. Lady Taylor in Bournemouth was the first to know:

I am now the owner of an estate upon Upolu, some two or three miles behind and above Apia... Three streams, two waterfalls, a great cliff, an ancient native fort, a view of the sea, and lowlands... are now mine. It would be affectation to omit a good many head of cattle; above all, as it required much diplomacy to have them thrown in, for the gentleman who sold to me was staunch. Besides all this, there is a great deal more forest than I have need for; or, to be plain, the whole estate is one impassable jungle which must be cut down and through at considerable expense. Then the house has to be built...

In February 1890 Stevenson wrote to Charles Baxter telling him that he had spent £450 on the land and it would need twice that to build a decent house on the difficult site. Even so, he was optimistic:

When we get the house built, the garden laid, and cattle in the place it will be something to fall back on for shelter and food; and if the island could stumble into political quiet, it is conceivable it might even bring in a little income... five streams, waterfalls, precipices, profound ravines, rich tablelands... There is my livelihood, all but books and wine.

A Sydney architect was engaged but his estimate of costs was exactly twice theirs, so he was allowed to go and costs were looked at again. Finally, work got underway. The locals couldn't understand why any house should require a fireplace – and a brick one at that. It would be the only one in the South Pacific. Fanny couldn't tell them it was needed to dry Louis's sheets after his night sweats, and Stevenson himself wouldn't admit that he wanted a fireplace to sit beside at night, as he loved to do after dinner in the evening – a sentiment that would set him back an extra thousand dollars. Whatever his growing affection for Samoa, nostalgia for Scotland could always catch him unawares, even as Villa Vailima began to take shape. There was no stopping the process now. There is something ominous about any kind of proprietorship, especially when one has to rely entirely on a third party, but Harry Moors was an ally from the start and Stevenson felt he could trust him and his alcoholic master carpenter to put up a house for the price originally discussed – twelve thousand dollars. It was to cost nearer twenty, and more than a hundred a week to keep up. But it was going to happen.

Cutting an idiosyncratic figure as the landed resident in his shabby white suit and yachting cap, he remained at heart the strolling player who had worn the velvet jacket in Edinburgh, the Inverness cape in Paris and the fur coat in Saranac Valley. He was still performing extempore in the theatre of his own circle. (That favourite velvet jacket was his motley, and he was never to discard it.) Whatever the situation he played his part, confident of the effect he created. It was as if he made a deliberate drama out of his own life – always being sure to cast himself in the lead. He may have only have played the penny whistle, as he termed his flageolet, but he rarely played second fiddle.

The urgency of his need for material gave a dramatic impetus to nearly everything he did. All his actions had theatrical dash and when he decided to settle in Samoa, most of the Savile circle took it to be a histrionic gesture of exile: Colvin prematurely mourned the loss to literature of a supreme essayist; Gosse said England had lost a great novelist; Lang regretted the poet that might have been. Henry James believed that Stevenson might have made a great military historian. None of them thought anyone literary could survive so far from Charing Cross Road. All roads, as far as they were concerned, led *to* London, not *from* it.

Stevenson explained his feelings in a further letter to Lady Taylor:

> I do feel as if I was a coward and a traitor to desert my friends; only, my dear lady, you know what a miserable corrhyzal (is that how you spell it?) creature I was at home; and here I have some real health. I can walk, I can ride, I can stand some exposure, I am up with the sun, I have real enjoyment of the world and of myself; it would be hard to be back again in England and to bed... I think it would be silly. I am sure it would and yet I feel shame...

His old friends seemed to have forgotten that sickness for him meant pain and 'deprivation of all that makes animal life desirable'. It was now clearly apparent that if Samoa agreed with him, he agreed with Samoa. He was at the beginning of a very meaningful relationship with the place and its people.

Whatever disadvantages his self-imposed exile might have on his literary life, he was here, and here he would remain, until 'that Unknown Steersman, whom we call God brings the boat round and safely into harbour'. He did not think about God much, but he felt that there was something – something ghostly – walking alongside him through life, like a spectral dog. He had a strong spiritual sense, but the practical man was to the fore – 'though we steer after a fashion yet we must sail according to the winds and currents'.

There was no way Stevenson could work among the hammers and saws and the workers' bird-like chatter. Having time and American dollars available, Mr and Mrs Stevenson, with the ever-present Lloyd, boarded the SS *Lübeck* for a trip to Sydney. It was on this voyage that he wrote memorably to Charles Baxter:

Do you remember – can we 'er forget?
How, in the coiled perplexities of youth,
In our wild climate, in our scowling town,
We gloomed and shivered, sorrowed, sobbed and feared!
The belching winter wind, the missile rain,
The rare and welcome silence of the snows,
The laggard morn, the haggard day, the night,
The grimy spell of the nocturnal town,
Do you remember...?

He got off to a bad start on this visit to Sydney. The Victoria Hotel in King Street, one of Sydney's grandest, had given the Stevensons a small room on the fourth floor instead of a suite of rooms on the first. One can hardly blame the desk clerk. When a long-haired, skeletal man and a woman in a straw hat shuffled into the foyer looking like frayed beachcombers, trailing luggage comprised of boxes tied with rope, tree-trunk buckets, palm-leaf baskets and rolls of tapa cloth, he naturally assumed that they didn't 'belong' at the Victoria. They were dispatched to the carpetless fourth floor – and none of the porters would touch the 'luggage'. The unfortunate desk clerk was treated to one of the famous Stevenson 'purples' – tirades in which words and meaning fused like arrows and went straight to the mark. Fanny had been on the receiving end of these many times. She could give nearly as good as she got but the poor desk clerk could only stand there with his mouth open. The scene attracted a crowd of staff and guests and the situation was only saved by the arrival of Belle and Lloyd.

Lloyd had gone immediately from the ship to see his sister at Miss Leaney's, her lodging house in Wooloomooloo, an unfashionable quarter favoured by artists and theatricals. They arrived at the Victoria in time to see their stepfather in the middle of one of his best *performances*. Despite herself, Belle was impressed. Few people can find the right word at the right time when they are upset or emotional but Stevenson had the knack, in the heat of a great temper, of keeping an ice-cool centre from which the words issued in a lethal volley. However, on this occasion, he was so taken aback at seeing Belle push her way through the onlookers, that he stopped at once and some sort of calm was restored.

Mother and daughter then took over. In no time they had the celebrated author and the luggage installed to his satisfaction in a whole floor of rooms in the less fashionable Oxford Hotel just across the road. The manager of the Victoria, belatedly realising Stevenson's identity (his name was on the front page of every Sydney newspaper), arrived the following day offering profuse apologies and a first-floor suite at half rate. Stevenson took some delight in declining, and even more in the fact that the Victoria had to send his copious mail over to the Oxford every day – 'in wicker baskets'.

No sooner had he unpacked than he took to his bed again with headache and loss of appetite, which developed into a fever which brought on a cough, which spattered blood on the sheets again. A Doctor Ross was called in. He recommended a move to the greater seclusion of the Union Club in Bligh Street. Even family visitors would have to be male at the gentlemen's club. Neither Stevenson nor Fanny seemed unduly upset at their forced separation. The only thing that annoyed him was that he wasn't allowed to play his flageolet in his room because 'it might disturb the other members'. Undeterred, he worked on *The Wrong Box* with Lloyd, sometimes getting up to sit by the window reading or, a novelty for him, to answer the telephone. One day he got a call from Dr Scot-Skirving, a friend from university days. Needless to say, he was invited up at once. Not long after this visit, Scot-Skirving again met Stevenson walking slowly up the King Street incline having just been to Angus and Robertson's bookshop to look for the latest Henry James. He said that he was devoting himself to writing a libel, 'a justified and righteous one.

This was a reference to his *Open Letter* which had been provoked by remarks he had heard at a Presbyterian church about the Reverend Dr Hyde's scurrilous private letter regarding Father Damien, the leper-priest. Written in the 'excellent, civilized, antipodean club smoking room' on 25 February, Stevenson's famous 'Open Letter to the Rev. Dr Hyde of Honolulu' was originally sent to the *Sydney Morning Herald,* which refused to print it. The *Australian Star* eventually did so, but only after it had appeared in Edinburgh's *Scots Observer.* It was so candid about the Protestant missionary doctor that Stevenson risked being sued for libel, but Hyde wisely took no action. When the letter was published by Scribner's as a pamphlet, Stevenson directed the royalties to the lepers at Molokai.

Despite this furore, he enjoyed Sydney and made some new friends, including Bertram Wise, Julian Ashton and Professor Anderson Stuart. But his health was poor.

> This visit to Sydney has smashed me handsomely... I made myself prisoner here in the club upon my first arrival. This is not encouraging for future ventures.

Belle now delivered his mail to the club and took his letters for posting. She was even allowed to go up to his room, where she usually found him propped up on pillows, writing to one of his many correspondents. One afternoon two housemaids were parading before him showing off their best dresses, all ready for the Servants' Ball to be held that evening in the town.

He was always one to notice the girls, whether in Pittenweem or Papeete, Hamburg or Honolulu, Swanston or Samoa. Nowadays it rarely went further than a twinkling observation. Fanny saw to that.

She was staying with Belle at the Leaney boarding house, a situation she found uncomfortable because of the worsening tensions in the Strong marriage. 'Strong' it was not. As always, things were tight financially, despite the cheques from Stevenson and what Belle could earn through writing articles for the *Bulletin,* occasional modelling at the Art School and teaching dance. Austin was being affected by his parents' constant squabbling. The atmosphere must have made Fanny ponder on her own marriage.

Things had not been the same since they left America. All the cruising might have done Stevenson's health some good, but they seemed to have drifted apart. Salt water had got into the bearings

A view from Vailima. Painting by Joe Strong.

The whole family on the verandah at Vailima, 1892.
From left to right: Lloyd Osbourne, Margaret Stevenson, Belle Strong, RLS,
Austin Strong, Fanny Osbourne and Joe Strong.

Vailima at the start of 1893.

Louis with 'his women', Fanny, Belle and Aunt Maggie. Sydney 1893.

Vailima. A painting by Nerli.

Waikiki, Hawaii, in 1889.

Fanny learns to make kava in front of the famous fireplace.

Chief Mata'afa, a friend to Tusitala, 1893.

Portrait of a Samoan chief by Nerli.

Road of the Loving Heart. A painting by Nerli.

The feast at Vailima to mark the opening of the Road of the Loving Heart.

RLS dictating to his amanuensis, Belle Strong, in the library at Vailima.

Fanny Osbourne Stevenson, main beneficiary of the Stevenson estate.

Robert Louis Stevenson lying in state in the big hall at Vailima.

Stevenson's grave on Mt Vaiea 'under the wide and starry sky'.

Some of the Stevenson exhibits in The Writers' Museum, Edinburgh.

of their matrimonial engine and rust was starting to appear. At sea they shared a cabin but at soon as they were ashore he had wanted his own bed. He had the excuse of his health to claim that separate beds would be better for both of them – but surely not separate rooms? Next it might be separate lives. Then what would she do? She needed to keep him alive, as much for her own sake as for his.

At this point Lloyd was appointed to return to Britain, accompanied by a Mr King, to bring back Aunt Maggie and the furniture from Heriot Row and Bournemouth, an expensive round trip, but Margaret Stevenson needed an escort and the new house needed the furniture. Besides, Lloyd might as well be useful. All Fanny herself really wanted was to get back home to California. A 'Skerryvore' in Oakland would have been her ideal. Stevenson, however, had other ideas. His thoughts were turning back to the sea.

Fanny was instructed to find a ship to take them both home – to Samoa. There was a seamen's strike in Sydney, but she determinedly tramped round the docks till she found a vessel that was going to Samoa. She would have taken anything that floated in order to get him there. That's how she found the *Janet Nicholl*, a rigged steamer bound for Auckland, Apia, the Marshall Islands, Noumea and New Caledonia. At the unpretentious offices of Henderson and MacFarlane, Marine Traders, arrangements were quickly made to embark on what turned out to be their final cruise, from 11 April to 26 July 1890.

Somewhat to her own surprise, Belle was sorry to see her stepfather go. She and Joe saw them off:

We were heavy-hearted... Louis looked so ill we thought we would never see him again. It seemed terrible for him to be going away in that soppy ship with drunken men and inky-black savages, and I didn't like the thought of my mother being the only woman on board with not even Ah Fu to look after her.

Ah Fu had recently left the Stevenson entourage. Having changed his wages and bonus into gold pieces and sewn them into a money belt, he bowed his farewells, never to be seen again by any of them.

Belle's recollection continues:

> some half-naked black men carried [Stevenson] up the narrow gangway [and] a red-faced, red-bearded man, somewhat the worse for drink, lurched about the slippery deck making a nuisance of himself in his efforts to help.

This was the captain. He fell overboard twice, and was twice fished out. Belle remarked on what a handsome man he was, even when drunk and half-drowned. She was susceptible to attractive men.

Eventually they laid Stevenson out on a board, wrapped like a mummy in a blanket. Belle left with a last regretful look at her mother, sitting stoically beside her husband on the open deck. He seemed to be asleep.

To be feared of a thing and yet to do it,
is what makes the prettiest kind of man.
KIDNAPPED

CHAPTER THIRTEEN

The Breakthrough

*What we want to see is one who can breast
into the world, do a man's work, and still
preserve his first and pure enjoyment of life.*
Henry David Thoreau

AFTER 'A CRUEL, rough, passage to Auckland', Stevenson spent the
day in his cabin and Fanny went ashore with one of the passengers,
Jack Buckland, to do some shopping. Buckland, known to all as
'Tin Jack', was what Stevenson called a 'natural'. Childlike and ap-
pealing, though annoying at times, he was a South Seas trader who
thought nothing of spending his whole year's income on an annual
burst of dissipation in Sydney. When, not long after this voyage, he
was swindled out of his money by a friend, he 'blew out what little
brains he possessed'. Stevenson had found him amusing company,
especially when he recited Shakespeare loudly and wrongly.

William Seed made the journey from Wellington to see Stevenson
and tried to persuade him to settle in New Zealand but, to his great
disappointment, it was clear that Stevenson was not interested, for all
that New Zealand might have to offer in the way of 'bookstores, white
table cloths and special wines'. He preferred to keep chasing the sun
'as it goes down and as it rises'. Who knows, the world being round,
his travels might bring him back to Britain, 'even if only to die'.

As it happened, he did almost die just a few days later, hardly
out of Auckland harbour. Tin Jack had returned to the *Janet Nicholl*
with a box of fireworks and cartridges with which he intended to
amuse his fellow-passengers. The ship had just got out into the bay
when the fireworks, which had been stored in the saloon, blew up.
Blue, green and red rockets exploded all over the deck and what

Fanny called 'gorgeous flames' rose up everywhere, as well as 'a most horrible chemical stench'. The captain and crew seemed transfixed at this unexpected pyrotechnic display; Fanny, ever resourceful, seized a blanket and tackled the fire on deck. The captain collected his wits and crawled on his belly through the dense smoke into the saloon and finally got the hose on the seat of the blaze. It took days to get the smoke out of his lungs. Had the winds been in another quarter or had the flames got to the cartridges, the whole ship would have gone up. Stevenson described it all as a 'pantomime'.

> Let no man say I am unscientific. When I ran, on the alert, out of my stateroom, and found the main cabin incarnadined with the glow of the last scene of a pantomime. I stopped dead: 'What is this?' said I. 'This ship is on fire, I see that; but why a pantomime?' And I stood and reasoned the point until my head was so fuddled by the fumes I could not find the companion... Lloyd lost most of his clothes and a great part of our photographs was destroyed. Fanny saw the natives tossing overboard a blazing trunk; she stopped them in time, and behold it contained my manuscripts...

This was a vital salvage on Fanny's part. She also saved their two cameras, though they lost most of the photographs and most of their clothes, which particularly upset Lloyd. Stevenson was remarkably sanguine about the whole episode. His manuscripts were safe. Words were his coinage – syllables could be reckoned in pennies, sentences sold at a shilling and paragraphs meant dollars. Words translated into income. Now that he had a commitment to wood and masonry as well as people, he would always have to have something sellable on the stocks.

Their first landfall was at Savage Island. As soon as the ship anchored, Stevenson went ashore and 'met gay islandresses who wrapped me in their embraces at the same time picking my pockets of all my tobacco'. On May Day they reached Apia and found, somewhat to Fanny's surprise, that work was going ahead at Vailima just as Moors had promised. Reassured, they re-embarked to head north-east for the Taukelas and Line Islands and another stop at Penrhyn, they then set course for the Ellice Islands and from there headed due north to the Gilberts. Everywhere they went, the impact of western civilisation was spelt out in sickness and disease among the local people, who lacked immunity to illnesses they had not previously been exposed to.

Altogether, the Stevenson party visited more that forty islands in less than four months. Louis remarked drily, 'hackney cabs have more variety than atolls'. They took King Tembinok aboard at Aranuka and gave him a lift back to Apemama. He brought his entire harem, bodyguard and royal entourage with him. It was an excuse for a party, but Stevenson paid for it with another visit from Bluidy Jack. Yet he remained optimistic, writing to Colvin:

> The truth is, I fear, this life is the only one that suits me; so long as I cruise in the South Seas I shall be well and happy – alas, no, I do not mean that, and *absit omen*! – I mean that, as soon as I cease from cruising, the nerves are strained, the decline commences, and I steer slowly... bedward.

The letters continued non-stop. Just off Peru Island in the Kingsmills Group, on 13 July, he wrote to his American editor, EL Burlingame:

> I shall probably return to Samoa direct, having given up all idea of returning to civilisation in the meantime. There, on my ancestral acres which I purchased six months ago from a blind Scots blacksmith, you will please address me until further notice...

When they reached Noumea, Stevenson was put ashore for a week's rest while Fanny and Lloyd continued on to Sydney; from there, Lloyd would go on to Edinburgh, as arranged. Stevenson advised Baxter, 'He is not – well – he is not a man of business – but, pray keep him in funds – if I have any; if I have not, pray try to raise them.' His old friend duly obliged.

Stevenson's letters from Noumea tell us that he was feeling 'very seedy, utterly fatigued and overborne with sleep'. But after a few days of his own company he was well enough to attend the Governor's reception, wearing borrowed and hastily-altered dress clothes: 'Anything else would indicate a want of respect.' He was ever the gentleman.

When he reached Sydney, he installed himself once again at the Union Club. Julian Ashton saw him there:

> I saw Stevenson again on his second visit when he spent a good deal of his time in bed, his strength having been sapped by a long attack of his pulmonary trouble. I often went to see him and usually found him hard at work lying down. His hours of work were from eight to twelve after which, if he felt well enough, he went abroad.

On this occasion he was on the lookout for anything by Kipling, his latest favourite – 'The fairy-godmothers were all tipsy at his christening.' In his opinion, 'Kipling has all the gifts. The question is what will he do with them?' Stevenson made sure he kept up with all 'the young ones'.

As he prepared to make his final landfall, he wrote to friends as if he were deliberately cutting the ties that bound him to his former life:

> I suppose we shall never see each other again. I shall never see whether you have grown older and you shall never deplore... that I have declined into a pantalooned Tusitala. Perhaps it is better so.

And, as if seeking a good exit line:

> I am fasting from all but sin... These last two years I have been much at sea and I have never wearied... and never once did I lose my fidelity to blue water and a ship. It is plain, then,

that my exile to a place of schooners and islands can in no sense be regarded as a calamity... Goodbye just now; I must take a turn at my proofs.

Fanny must have noticed how companionable Belle and Stevenson were becoming. Belle accompanied him on his rare forays out of the Club, and on one of these expeditions they had a major breakthrough in their relationship. They had a real heart-to-heart, their first-ever. Belle was at the end of her tether with Joe, who had managed to sell some painting then blew the proceeds on fripperies and drink. Stevenson's opinion of Joe is made clear in a letter to Baxter:

O Christ Jesus! It is sometimes too much to have to support this creature... for he owes me his body, his soul and his boots, and the soup that he wipes on his moustache... Hard is the lot of him who has dependents.

But he did see it as his duty to support Belle, who was his wife's flesh and blood.

For nearly six months, Belle has been a hitherto unheard-of model of gratitude; by which I mean, she has never said a word of thanks; but gone ahead, and managed the money the way I wished her to, and met my views in every way in her power, against all obstacles.

It was in this unprecedented state of truce that they now talked together as never before. Stevenson suggested that she and Austin come to stay at Vailima, but she was worried about bringing up her son on a remote tropical island. They discussed Austin at length, but the real problem was Joe. The old enmity and mistrust between Belle and Stevenson finally evaporated. He continued to urge her to come to Samoa, saying that the new house needed young life in it. He pointed out that while her mother might act as if she were indestructible, she was not. She would like to have her daughter near her.

In September 1890 Stevenson and Fanny returned to Apia on the *Lübeck*. The Strongs did not join them. Belle said that she needed time to think. Stevenson may have wondered if he had said too much – or not enough? However, other matters claimed his attention.

While Fanny bullied the domestic staff into her way of working and even with the din of building in his ears, Stevenson put in some solid work on his three current projects – *Island Nights' Entertainments* (almost completed), *The Wrecker* (completed but needing polishing) and *The Ebb-Tide*, a new novel just started. An out-of-the-way corner on the top floor was made available for him and a writing desk was improvised from cuts of timber.

Even in these circumstances, the Stevensons still had visitors. One, the Harvard historian Henry Brooks Adams, described the emerging Vailima as 'a two-storey Irish shanty' and the Stevensons as, 'so thin and emaciated that he looked like a bundle of sticks in a bag... [and] a woman in the usual missionary nightgown that was no cleaner than her husband's shirt and drawers.'

He omitted to mention that they had been trying to clean a black-leaded stove on the day he arrived. However, he added, 'Though I could not forget the dirt and the squalor, I found Stevenson extremely entertaining...' And, as an afterthought, 'His face has a certain beauty, especially the eyes, but it is the beauty of disease.'

Towards the end of 1890, walking through the forest now being cleared around the house, Stevenson had an idea for a new story.

> It shot through me like a bullet in one of my moments of awe, alone in that tragic jungle... very strange, very extravagant... varied and picturesque... [it] has a pretty love affair, and ends happily.

He started, stopped, started again, then left it, but by the end of the following year it was with McClure as a serial called *The Beach of Falesà*, which has come to be recognised as a minor masterpiece of South Seas writing. It was a breakthrough for Stevenson: in it his lovers sleep together without being married, albeit with a marriage certificate especially faked for the night. This was a new Stevenson at work, no longer afraid to undo a few buttons. However, when the *Illustrated London News* ran the story in 1892, the editor, Clement Shorter omitted the controversial section. Mention of two little children 'wriggling out of their clothes and running away, mother-naked,' was also cut. Stevenson was understanding:

> Some of the greatest things in literature cannot be published in journals for general family reading, and no editor who knows his business would worry himself about the feelings of an author, however great, when he had such a point for decision.

After each morning's work, Stevenson would walk in the jungle that surrounded Vailima.

> My long silent contests in the forest have had a strange effect on me. The unconcealed vitality of these vegetables, their exuberant number and strength, the attempts – I can use no other word – of the llianas to enwrap and capture the intruder, the awful silence, the knowledge that all my efforts are only like the performance of an actor, a thing of a moment...

He had to cope with Fanny's performances however, and when these became intolerable he would jump on his New Zealand pony, Jack, bought from a circus that found itself stranded at Apia, and gallop down to spend a night of gossip and ghost-stories with Harry Moors. They had Christmas dinner there, along with a well-known murderer and his wife, which would have intrigued Stevenson but Fanny, blaming her foul mood on earache, spoiled the occasion for everyone.

Margaret Stevenson was due to arrive in Sydney on 18 January 1891. Fanny could not face the sea passage and so Stevenson decided to go alone. He did not have a good journey. The *Lübeck* broke down off Fiji and had to resort to sail, which meant no Auckland visit, as planned. Worse, he was unable to meet his mother off the *Lusitania*. The upset brought on another visitation from Bluidy Jack and Maggie brought her son ashore and straight into a Sydney boarding house where she could look after him herself. Lloyd, meantime, hurried back to Samoa, accompanied by his new friend, Mr King. Stevenson vented his frustration in a letter to Colvin:

> It is vastly annoying that I can't even go to Sydney without an attack, and heaven knows my life was anodyne. I only once dined with anybody; at the club with Wise; worked all morning, a terrible dead pull; a month only produced the imperfect embryos of two chapters; lunch at the boarding house, played on my pipe, went out and did some of my messages; dined at a French restaurant, and returned to play draughts, whist and Van John with my family. This makes a cheery life after Samoa; but it isn't what you call burning the candle at both ends, is it?

What he did do, however, was have a second talk with Belle. She had made up her mind not to come to Samoa. That would seem to be that.

Margaret Stevenson's arrival in Apia was an event that drew people from all over Upolo. The tall, slim figure of Tom Stevenson's widow emerged majestically from the ship dressed in black with a white mantilla on her head. Soon it seemed as if the entire contents of Heriot Row had been disgorged in the sands of Apia. Mahogany and rosewood furniture, oil paintings and prints by the score, statues and busts, kitchenware, expensive glass of every kind, dishes, cutlery and casks of wine and a whole library of books. It took a regiment of bearers a day and a night to move it all up to the house on the hill. As the long procession wove up from the harbour like an ancient caravanserai, Stevenson delighted at the sight of so many familiar things.

He led his mother up on to the verandah of the still uncompleted house saying, 'Welcome home, Mama.' She, however, was not impressed with a bedroom with no ceiling and lavatory arrangements that depended on its not raining. After a few days, Margaret Stevenson decided that she was too old for camping and arrangements were made for her to sail to New Zealand to stay with relatives in Wellington until Vailima was ready.

Stevenson was still anxious about having to do something to stop the Strongs being such a constant drain on his dollars. He knew how much Fanny wanted her daughter and grandson near her. Joe could go to hell as far as she was concerned, but Stevenson, as head of the household, decided that the best thing would be to bring all three to Samoa. That way he could keep his eye on Mr Strong. The question was, would Belle come? Hadn't she said herself that she planned to leave Joe and make a life for herself in Sydney?

'She'll come,' said Fanny.

Aunt Maggie returned to Vailima during the second week in May, bringing with her a maid, Mary Carter, a sturdy Kiwi with an equally sturdy sense of humour. She would need it for dealing with Fanny. Everyone commented on how well Stevenson looked. He was enjoying the best health he had ever known.

Fanny must have worked hard on Belle: as she predicted, her daughter finally accepted their invitation. She, Joe and Austin were set to arrive *en famille* from Sydney. With the full cast assembled, the curtain could rise on the next phase of Stevenson's life drama:

the most beautiful adventures are not those we go to seek...
it is when you come back at nightfall and look into the familiar room, you may find love – or death – waiting beside the stove...

Happiness, at least, is not solitary;
it joys to communicate; it loves others;
for it depends on them for its existence.
Henry David Thoreau

CHAPTER FOURTEEN

The Speaking Chief

No class of man is altogether bad;
but each has its own faults and virtues.
KIDNAPPED

The name of the ancestral acres is going to be Vailima... The place is beautiful beyond dreams; some fifty miles of the Pacific spread in front; deep woods all round, a mountain making in the sky a profile of huge trees on our left; about us the little island of our clearing... It is a good place to be in; night and morning we have Theodore Rousseaus (always a new one) hung to amuse us on the walls of the world; and the moon makes the night a piece of heaven...

MANY OF STEVENSON's letters from Samoa are in this tone, ebullient and full of wonder, as if he couldn't believe his own luck. Letter-writing, for so long his leisure and pleasure while on the road and at sea, became almost a way of life now that he was landed gentry on top of his own hill. He was anchored permanently in a safe harbour but he still kept an eye out to sea. Opening letters assumed for him the importance of a religious rite. He awaited replies as if they were manna, which they were to a man who regarded friendship as the staple diet of existence. To receive letters, one first has to send them and this, now with Belle's help, he did assiduously.

With the letters, from complete strangers as much as from old friends, the foundations of the Tusitala legend were being laid as carefully and solidly as the foundations of any of his family's light-houses. Finding his sea legs, Stevenson had found his way to Samoa and in finding Vailima, he had re-discovered his body and in finding his body, he had finally found himself. The inveterate beachcomber had at last found a place that seemed to satisfy all his needs.

I am in the sea for hours, wading over my knees for shells; I have been five hours on horseback; this climate, these voyages, these landfalls at dawn; new islands peeping from the morning bank; new forested harbours; new passing alarms of squalls and surf – the whole tale of my life is better to me than any poem...

His identity in the northern hemisphere had been largely determined by his intellect, but now a new identity was made possible by a stronger sensual awareness and the release of his emotions. There was no rationalising here, it was wholly a matter of feeling, free at last of other people's idea of who he was, or who he ought to be. He could exult in the unexpected freedom of being well.

I have endured some two-and-forty years without public shame and had a good time as I did it. If only I could secure a violent death, what a fine success. I wish to die in my boots, no more land of counterpane for me – to be drowned, to be shot, to be thrown from a horse – even to be hanged, rather than pace again a slow dissolution by disease.

Though his books and articles guaranteed a substantial income, maintaining Vailima was a constant drain on funds and he could not stop worrying about money.

I am living patriarchally six hundred feet above the sea on the shoulder of a mountain. Behind me the bush slopes up to the backbone of the island... with no inhabitants save wild doves and flying foxes, many particoloured birds. many black and many white; a very eerie, dim, strange place and hard to travel... Is this not Babylon the Great I have builded? I call it Subpriorsford.

When he needed to lay down his pen for an hour, if only to re-fresh his eyes and his head, he found solace in 'the jungle', the belt of forest that surrounded the house. Wandering alone among the dark trees, he revelled in the stillness.

Here there are no trains, only men passing barefoot. No carts or carriages; at worst, the rattle of a horse's shoe among the rocks; beautiful silence...

The inveterate talker and performer needed time 'off-stage'. Stevenson's deepest religious feelings found silent expression in his cathedral forest, more so than on Sunday mornings when the Laird of Vailima led his household in prayer.

Belle Strong had vivid memories of her landfall at Apia at the end of May 1891. On her own admission, she fell in love with humid, sultry Samoa at first sight. She swore later she could smell it before she saw it. That smell of Samoa, a mix of ylang-ylang, wood-smoke and copra, had come drifting over the horizon to the *Lübeck* as she steamed towards the shore. She had hardly moored in the bay before Belle was over the side, climbing down the rope ladder into a whale-boat crewed by young men, their bronze skin glistening with coconut oil. She thrilled as the long boat went skimming past the great hulk of the *Adler*, which had been wrecked in a storm the year before, to slide swiftly and silently up to the recently built jetty. There was no carrying the passengers ashore now. Not that Belle would have minded.

Her first real look at the Samoans, 'God's best, his sweetest work', as Stevenson called them, was as seductive as the atmosphere. The males in *lavalavas* worn from their waists like kilts, the females wearing them from just above or just under their breasts, both sexes with flowers in their hair. The scents and smells were ravishing.

Sex permeated the atmosphere. Virtually every expatriate white man had a Samoan mistress. Their wives, not to be outdone, often made their own 'alternative arrangements'. Apia was hot, in every sense. Harry Moors, who managed several concurrent liaisons, was taken aback that Stevenson disapproved of promiscuity. His high-mindedness always took people by surprise. It was another of his contradictions.

In her memoir Belle describes her first approach to Vailima. Behind her in the line of ponies she could see Joe, looking sullen, with Cocky the parrot on his shoulder, was struggling with the box containing three cats brought to deal with the rats at the new house. Austin was being carried by Lloyd. Aunt Maggie on horseback and ahead was Louis, tanned and fit-looking. Was this her ailing stepfather? They went past the big houses of the white settlers. Beyond the straw huts at Tanugamanono they left the road and went up the track through the green chute of cleared jungle and she had her first glimpse of Mt Vaea rising into the bluest of skies. Climbing higher, round yet another bend, and there was Vailima.

It was a large wooden house with verandahs all round, painted peacock-blue and with a red roof. Massive ironwood and banyan trees stood sentinel before it. The party dismounted among the jasmine vines and walked across the lawn to the front porch. The splendour of the setting made Belle gasp. Cocky, now on her shoulder, immediately flew into one of the trees at the side of the house. Its hoarse squawk was the only sound as they paused for a moment on the front steps, gazing out to the ocean, entranced. Stevenson broke the golden silence, remarking with pride, 'Do you know, there is nothing between us and the South Pole.'

Fanny then bustled out. After embracing Belle and Austin and giving a token nod to Joe, she took charge in her usual peremptory manner. The Strongs were shown to Pineapple Cottage, where Fanny and Louis had first lived when they came to the island.

Joe and Belle were soon to discover that Vailima was no sleepy retreat. It was a veritable hive of industry, with Louis as Chairman of the Board and Fanny as General Manager. Everyone had a job to do. The Chairman set the pace by being up at dawn. He would write until breakfast on the porch. At seven, Lloyd took his clearing squad out into the jungle. Fanny was in charge of the garden and flouting the Samoan tradition that the kitchen was a male province, she decided the menus. Aunt Maggie had light domestic duties and shared young Austin's schooling with Lloyd. Joe was given the job of looking after the hens. As for Belle, she increasingly spent her days as Stevenson's secretary and dictation-taker.

From first light, Fanny could be seen toiling away in the garden, wearing a blue holaku. She liked getting her hands grimy with earth. Stevenson was right when he said she had the soul of a peasant. But the strain was telling. She was not her old, confident self, although she was still as assertively voluble as ever, and her voice was often raised, shrilly chastising her gardeners, Lafaele and Laulelu.

Seeing how closely Belle worked with Tusitala, many Samoans, especially those beyond the estate, thought that Fanny and Belle were his two wives. This fuelled Fanny's growing resentment at the amount of time Belle spent alone with her husband.

The first Stevenson story to be translated into Samoan was 'The Bottle Imp'. After its publication in the local missionary magazine, *O le Solu,* his ink bottle became an object of awe for his Samoan staff, who saw it as a magical fountain from which all his wealth flowed. They were not far wrong. Metaphorically at least, Tusitala, the teller of tales, did draw his strength from an ink bottle. With their traditional respect for oratory, the Samoans initiated Stevenson as a *Matai* or 'speaking chief' after only one year's residence on the island – honouring his brilliance as a storyteller. He became their true friend and champion.

Stevenson certainly had courage, both moral and physical. Nothing daunted the man. He allowed himself to get drawn into local politics despite the fact that he had no stomach for 'the only profession for which no preparation is thought necessary'. Fanny observed that in general terms he

sympathised with the socialist but saw no royal road for others by his own path. He believed he had no rights, only undeserved indulgences, but he must not eat unearned bread.

He must pay the world in some fashion for what it gave him – first materially, then in kindness, then in love. Too much ease frightened him. He occasionally insisted on some sharp discomfort to awaken him to realities.

Stevenson held every man to be 'his own judge and mountain-guide through life'. Essentially, he believed in the 'ultimate decency of things'. His ethical standard was simple honesty:

The profit for every act should be this, that it was right for us to do it... The first duty in this world is for a man to pay his way; when that is quite accomplished he may plunge into what eccentricity he likes but emphatically not till then.

As GB Stern said of Stevenson, if his early days were full of bravado, *all* his days were brave. He was now about to show his courage. Civil war threatened in Samoa, and even his writing was temporarily set aside so that he could give his full attention to 'this distracted archipelago of children set upon by a clique of fools'. Samoa was governed in a tripartite arrangement between the British, American and German consuls, none of whom represented the interest of the island as a whole. The rule of King Laupepa, a German puppet, was being challenged by Mata'afa, whom Stevenson openly favoured. To complicate matters, Mata'afa's Catholic faith did not put him in favour with the London Missionary Society and the Protestant establishment in consular circles. Stevenson, a natural outsider, actually got on better with the German and American consuls. He regarded politics as 'a vile and bungling business' that made 'honest men cunning and devious and clever men look like dolts'. Nevertheless, his sense of injustice gave him no option but to be involved. He explained to Andrew Lang:

I'm in a deuce of a flutter with politics, which I hate, and in which I certainly do not shine; but a fellow can't stand aside... 'taint decent... but it's a grind to be interrupted by midnight

messengers, and pass your days writing proclamations (which
are never proclaimed) and petitions (which ain't pettited) and
letters to *The Times* which it makes my jaws yawn to read.

Stevenson saw through the cynical game being played by white
factions at the expense of the Samoans. Germany wanted to
maximise its copra profits, America protected its whaling rights,
Britain defended its right to trade, the missionaries harvested souls.
Cusack-Smith, the British Consul, regarded the celebrated athor
as an interfering nuisance. Stevenson was unrepentant – but in
response to the deteriorating situation, he installed a rack of rifles
at Vailima. (Fanny, at least, knew how to use one.) He expressed
his views in a series of seven impassioned letters fired off to *The
Times* between February 1889 and May 1894. He was bitingly
critical of Germany's role. The British Colonial Office actually
considered deporting Stevenson, 'for his own safety'. He countered
with the suggestion that Cusack-Smith was the one who should be
deported. Sir John Thurston, the British High Commissioner in the
Western Pacific, introduced a *Regulation for the Maintenance of
Peace and Good Order in Samoa*, a device intended to control the
actions of British subjects in Samoa – in fact, little more than an
attempt to gag Stevenson. Stevenson would not be gagged. Colvin
in London put his case to Lord Rosebery, the Foreign Secretary.
This high-level lobbying paid off. British officials in the South Seas
were reprimanded and ordered to leave 'the distinguished author'
alone. A combination of deference to celebrity and political ex-
pediency had won the day. For an avowed non-politician, he
had not done too badly.

Stevenson organised a meeting of all parties, hoping to obtain
democratic concessions from the German authorities, including the
ruthlessly self-interested trading company, the Deutsche Koloniale
Gesellschaft. Integral to his vision was the recognition of Mata'afa
as rightful king. Lloyd Osbourne commented:

Samoa filled his need for the dramatic... He expanded on its teeming stage where he could hold warriors in leash and play Richelieu to half-naked kings.

Vailima came into its own as a splendidly theatrical setting for gatherings: the redwood walls of its great hall glowing in shaded light, the silver gleaming and the glass glittering, the imported furniture standing haughtily on straw mats spread out on the wooden floor. The Samoan servants wore flowers in their hair and lavalavas in Stewart tartan. Aunt Maggie would sit, her back ramrod straight, while Fanny scrutinised everything from under permanently knitted brows. Meanwhile Belle, odalisque, reclined exotically on cushions. On these 'Vailima nights', Samoan and European guests mingled and hospitality was dispensed with considerable élan – and even more considerable expense. Fanny and Belle saw to that. The two Americans were heroic party-givers, and watching them organse it all so efficiently, the Samoans could not be persuaded that Tusitala did not have two wives.

I do not care two straws for all the nots.
ETHICAL STUDIES

CHAPTER FIFTEEN

Less Afraid of a Petticoat

When the present is so exacting
who can annoy himself about the future?
TRAVELS WITH A DONKEY

BELLE WAS A whole new woman once she was free at last of Joseph
Dwight Strong. He was discovered helping himself to the whisky
in the store through the use of a duplicate key. He had also been
pocketing the money given for chicken-feed and spending it on
Faauma, a beautiful Vailima maid. When Strong began openly
'decorating the beach' at Apia with her, Stevenson acted at once,
and threw him out of the house.

After Belle had secured a divorce, Lloyd was instructed to deliver
young Austin to his Aunt Nellie Sanchez in Monterey, who had recently become a widow. This was Stevenson's way of helping Belle
out and putting distance between Austin and his drunken father.
The money Stevenson sent her would keep them both until Austin
was old enough to go to Stanford University or get a job. Till then
he could return to Vailima in the holidays to see his mother and
grandmother. Lloyd, as always, was glad of the chance of another
Pacific voyage and an extended stay in San Francisco, well away
from the sweat and toil of Vailima. He was under orders to meet
Graham Balfour, who was coming out from Edinburgh, and bring
him on to Vailima by the first ship.

Aunt Maggie was very proud of Graham, the future Oxford don
who would become his famous cousin's first biographer. She liked
having him at her elbow at dinner, even if he had to jack-knife his
lanky frame in order to sit cross-legged on the verandah floor. The
house staff couldn't pronounce the name Graham, so he became

Palema to them and then, much to his amusement, to everybody else. Palema was popular with everyone in the house. He was also unmarried, and that was his biggest attraction as far as Fanny was concerned. She thought he would make an ideal match for Belle now that she was a free woman again. Belle liked the easy-going Scot at once but he was altogether too bland for her taste. Louis's cousin was like all the Balfours, clever and charming but diffident to the point of being otiose. Graham seemed terrified by Fanny and was shy with Belle. When he wasn't involved in building work with Lloyd and Lafaele, or with his cousin in noisy games of chess, he tended to be more with his Aunt Maggie, who was without a companion now that Mary Carter had left.

Every morning Belle was seeing Stevenson at his best, which was when he was working. Telling his stories. And telling them first *to her*. She found herself looking forward to their daily sessions. She felt she shared his creativity with him, not only with his letters, which tended to be left until the afternoon, but in the *real* work of the morning. He had actually asked her to help him with *Prince Otto*. She could feel herself responding to him more and more each day. It wasn't difficult, he was a lovely, funny, charming, tender man – when he wanted to be.

It may have been mere coincidence, but from this time on Stevenson's writing became freer, looser, less inhibited, more *adult*. Whether this was due to Belle's influence, or even the mere fact of her proximity, or just sheer practice as he always insisted, is a moot point, but there is no doubt that his writing changed:

> As for women, I am no more in fear of them:I can do a sort alright. Age makes me less afraid of a petticoat, but I am a little in fear of grossness... This has kept me off the sentiment hitherto, and now I am to try...

The 'try' resulted in his best female characters, Catriona Drummond and Miss Grant of Prestongrange ('I think some day I must marry Miss Grant.'). Both featured in *Catriona* (originally entitled

David Balfour) 'I shall never do a better book', he said. It was written during a burst of energy between March and July 1892. Stevenson was delighted.

> *Beach of Falesà* and *Catriona* seem to me nearer what I mean than anything I have ever done; nearer what I mean by fiction; the nearest thing before was *Kidnapped...*

This was Stevenson at the top of his form and at the peak of his health. There was a happy conjoining of physical well-being and a creative surge, and Belle was there to witness it daily. She could not have been anything but impressed.

Beyond the confines of the writing-room and the supper-table, Stevenson had become something of a hero-figure, a Samoan lion – and one that occasionally showed its claws, as Joe Strong could testify. RLS had drawn some international curiosity with his recent political efforts and, because of this, another woman now came in his life, albeit briefly. A woman as colourful as any he might have created in his new certainty. This was the 'Queen of Sydney', Margaret Villiers, Countess of Jersey. As Stevenson put it, 'a little adventure into the *Waverley Novels'* was about to begin.

Margaret Elizabeth Leigh was married to Victor Albert George Childe Villiers, the 7th Earl of Jersey, Governor of New South Wales. She was the darling of Sydney society. Her brother Captain Rupert Leigh was a friend of Bazett Haggard, brother of the author Rider Haggard. Bazett, the British Land Commissioner, was a friend and ally of Stevenson's.

When Captain Leigh was invited to Samoa, Lady Jersey seized the chance to meet Stevenson. In August 1892 she came ashore at Apia with her brother and an entourage which included her daughter, Lady Margaret, known as Markie. Lady Jersey recalled in her memoirs:

> I shall never forget the moment when I first saw him and his

wife standing at the door of the long, wood-panelled room in Ruge's Building. A slim, dark-haired, bright-eyed figure in a loose black velvet jacket over his white vest and trousers, and a scarlet silk sash. By his side the short, dark woman with cropped, curly hair and the strange piercing glance...

No doubt, had looks been able to kill, Lady Jersey would have died on the spot. Fanny disliked her from the start, describing her in her diary as

tall and leggy and awkward, with bold black eyes and sensual mouth; very selfish and greedy of admiration, a touch of vulgarity, courageous as a man and reckless as a woman.

Despite having been uncomfortable with women characters in his books, Stevenson was always comfortable with them in life. He liked all kinds of women, at every kind of level, of that we are sure. But it genuinely took him aback how much they liked *him*. He took to Lady Jersey immediately – to him she was admirable, unfussy, plucky and kind. They got to know each other at a dinner given by 'King' Laupepa in her honour. No doubt everyone present took the chance to put their point of view to the influential visitor, who could advance their cause outside Samoa, if only in New South Wales. Stevenson made his pitch for 'King' Mata'afa. Lady Jersey was intrigued. She evidently shared his taste for adventure and they hatched a plan to make a clandestine visit to Mata'afa that would not have been out of place in the most picaresque of his novels; for a time, he was Alan Breck in the South Seas, and she was the Misses Drummond and Grant combined. There was an air of romance over the whole escapade but, despite his playfulness, Stevenson was fully aware of the possible consequences, speculating whether news of it might even trigger war. None the less, he loved every minute of it, confessing, 'the thing wholly suits my book and fits my predilection for Samoa'.

Haggard and Leigh took the view that Lady Jersey could not

openly meet the 'rebel', particularly after having been honoured by the opposing faction. It was Stevenson's suggestion that she go as 'Miss Amelia Balfour', supposedly Graham's sister. Their ambassadorial project had the ring of a 'good jape' about it. The Jersey party visited Vailima to discuss the plan and were mightily impressed. Fanny did not reciprocate the sentiment. 'A selfish, champagne Charley set,' she wrote in her diary. There was a lot of laughter and silly talk. Fanny made it clear she would have nothing to do with the whole business and retired to her room saying she wasn't feeling well. She said pointedly that she had to oversee the installation of the new bathhouse and couldn't spare the time. Nor did she think Stevenson should go, anticipating, incorrectly for once, that he would suffer for it afterwards. The truth was that it was she who was suffering. She was displaying symptoms of the acute manic depression that was to dog her final years in Samoa. it was noted that Stevenson often seemed relieved to get away from her.

Aunt Maggie briskly made the point that it was perhaps unfitting for Lady Jersey's daughter to travel in such wild country. She had done it herself, and declared it 'no picnic'. Yet it was plain, she added, that the Countess required a lady companion. Belle volunteered, which was quite a surprise given that she had hitherto shown no great appetite for exertion.

A few days later, on Sunday 14 June, Stevenson sent his partner-in-crime a playful note suggesting they rendezvous at the Gasi-gasi water when the 'King over the water – the Gasi-gasi water – will be pleased to see the clan of Balfour mustering so thick around his standard'; further evoking the spirit of Jacobite adventure, he dated the letter 1745.

The party set off at first light, mounted on ponies, leaving the Vailima ark two by two. A posse of servants ran alongside, carrying everything the riders would need, including a box of 'shop cigarettes' and a bottle of whisky as a present for Mata'afa. Stevenson led off on Jack, with 'Amelia' beside him. 'Miss Osbourne' followed on her favourite brown mare, Peggy, with Rupert Leigh holding the lead rein. Bazett and Graham brought up the rear. Lloyd, Markie and Austin came out to see them off. Stevenson gave a little wave to Fanny who glowered from an upstairs window. Lady Jersey noticed but said nothing.

'Come then, Amelia!' called Stevenson, and they were off. They followed Mata'afa's two guides up narrow mountain paths between the 'huge vegetables', as Stevenson called the trees. His constant flow of conversation, delivered with the dynamism of a professional entertainer, captivated Lady Jersey.

The detail of what happened during this expedition is open to speculation. Belle makes no mention of it in her recollections, *This Life I Have Loved*. Stevenson himself hardly recorded his own impressions although he did contribute to a pamphlet entitled *An Object of Pity, or, The Man Haggard*, a curious compilation from several hands, which satirised the good-natured Haggard, who took it all in good part. Stevenson, however, did take the opportunity to re-evaluate Belle: 'Never says please or thankyou for anything, but shows a brave face to the world. She is my wife's daughter, my secretary, my amanuensis, my woman-Friday on my desert island, my finder of things, my last assistance, my oasis, my staff of hope, my grove of peace, my anchor, my haven in a storm. She's Belle, I suppose.'

How strange that we should all, in our unguarded moments, rather like to be thought a bit of a rogue with the women.
AN INLAND VOYAGE

CHAPTER SIXTEEN

Against the Tide

Now they were to return like voyagers in the play,
to see what rearrangements Fortune had perfected,
what surprises stood ready at home, and whither
and how far the world had travelled in their absence...
AN INLAND VOYAGE

A PLAGUE OF influenza devastated Samoa in the first month of 1893. Remarkably, Stevenson was the last to succumb at Vailima and it brought on another attack of 'Bluidy Jack'. Stevenson lost his voice and had to use deaf-and-dumb sign language, learned from Belle, in order to keep working on *Weir of Hermiston*.

Fanny was as low in health, both physically and mentally as she had ever been. A holiday in Sydney was proposed and bookings made for Stevenson and his 'three ladies' on the *Mariposa*.

In the last week of February, they put in at Auckland. There, Stevenson met Sir George Grey, the Governor of New Zealand, to whom he outlined the complexities of the political situation in Samoa. Grey's concern was how German and American machinations in Samoa might affect New Zealand. According to Belle's notes of the meeting, he advised Stevenson:

pay no attention to attacks, go on doing what you're doing for the good of Samoa; the time will come when it is appreciated, and I am one of the few men who have lived long enough to learn this... The worst of my anxiety is over. I thought you were an invalid. When I see the fire in your eyes, your life, your energy, I feel no more anxiety for Samoa... You may have thought you stopped at Samoa on a whim... but

I believe in Providence. There is something over us; and when I heard that a man with the romantic imagination of a novelist had settled down on one of those island, I said to myself, these races will be saved!

After a congenial talk on literature the two men walked arm in arm to the front door of the hotel, like an 'ancient schoolboy walking with a younger boy'. Stevenson wrote:

It makes a man small, and the extent to which he approved of what I had done – or rather, have tried to do – encouraged me. Sir George is an expert at least. He knows these races. He is not a small *employé* with an ink-pot and a *Whitaker*.

The writer and politician treated each other with full respect and Sir George, very much a bookman in his own right, ordered the Edinburgh Edition of Stevenson's *Works* after the writer continued on his voyage. At Sydney docks, reporters and cameramen thronged at the dockside to meet him. Though he generally disliked meeting the press, he was glad to take this opportunity to disprove reports of his death which had been circulating prior to his arrival. The *Sydney Morning Herald* reported:

His physique is vastly improved since his last visit... Today he is well set-up, has the glow of health in his countenance, and altogether bears testimony to the beneficent effects of the Samoan climate...

What had not improved, however, was his diplomatic skills. His political comments were expressed in terms 'rather too plain for publication in Australia'. Otherwise, the paper was fulsome in its praise:

The personality of a famous writer is always interesting to his readers – and who is not a reader of Stevenson's enthralling books? Mr Stevenson may still be called a young man. He is tall and thin, and walks with a slight stoop of the shoulders. His face is refined and beautiful. Looking on it, one would at once say, 'This is a man of intellect', but looking into the full, glowing dark eyes, one would go further and say, 'This is a man of genius'.

This unctuous testimonial probably did little to improve Stevenson's opinion of journalists.

At a meeting of the Women's South Seas Missionary Association held at Quong Tart's Rooms, Margaret Stevenson read a paper by her son on the need to preserve local culture and customs while evangelising according to Christian practices – enlightened advice that has taken more than a hundred years to be generally accepted. The talk was written up in *The Presbyterian*, to which Stevenson gave two further interviews in which he expressed his views on the misuse of black labour in the sugar fields of Queensland and the 'unvisored' kidnapping of young men from the South Sea islands for that purpose:

On the whole, the influence of whites in the islands strikes me as far from beneficial, and the more whites, the worse is the effect. A single trader, even the most atrocious scoundrel, is rapidly conquered by his medium, adopts Island civility, even if he had none of his own when he came there. But as soon as the whites are in a considerable body, the work of de-civilization proceeds merrily. I said 'de-civilization' but, if you insist on it, I will say 're-barbarization'. At least it is a process towards the worse.

Once again, he was swimming against the tide. Reports of his radical views were largely confined to the pages of the *Presbyterian*. His daily writing stint was generally done at the Union Club. Tighe Ryan of the *Antipodean* found him in his lodgings,

snugly ensconsed in an easy chair, one leg on the other, a book on his knee, and a smoking cigarette in his right hand which hung loosely over the arm of the chair. A glass of sherry was within reach... and wreaths of light blue smoke were filling the room. He had just risen from his afternoon nap, he said, and sleep was still in his head. I carried away in my mind that evening recollection of a soft, low, but clear voice, with the slight Scottish accent... the rare gesture; the thin, bronzed face, changing with every mood, the fine sparkling eyes so far apart, the active figure, so sparse that in a wind storm it might require the leaden shoes of Philetus.

He was inundated with invitations to speak, from every kind of self-important institution (though he said, 'I'd have walked ten miles to speak to an infants' school'). He was made a member of the Thistle Club, as the Reverend Will Burnett recorded:

Height, over medium but increased by extreme thinness, a magician who drew him to your heart as well as your eyes. Your eyes sought joy in his. No portrait or photograph portrays those eyes. Some make them flat and far apart, some make them 'sleekit'. The charm of them dispelled all critical faculty... In soft neck-wear and velvet jacket. Placed two hands in respective pockets, took himself in charge and gradually tightened his grip... in happiest vein himself and spread happiness all around.

On 14 March he made a 'delightful and witty speech' at the Australia Hotel and two days later he was the guest of the Cosmopolitan Club, where he spoke of his beloved France. One of the guests commented, 'I've never seen a man who looked so ill speak so well'. He visited Sydney University, where he signed the Visitors' Book. Later that day, he and Belle went off to an artists' colony at Balmoral where they enjoyed a convivial evening. One of the artists he may have met there was the Italian-Australian painter Count Nerli. However, Nerli may have chosen to keep out of Stevenson's way. On a visit to Vailima in 1892 he had painted one of the best Stevenson portraits, capturing something of the author's inner vigour. But because Fanny didn't like it, Stevenson did not buy it. He nevertheless made up an amiable verse on Nerli and they parted as friends. On his return to Sydney, Nerli made several copies of his portrait. (These have found their way into various collections, including the Scottish National Portrait Gallery and the Writers' Museum in Edinburgh.) Even the highly moral Stevenson might not have disapproved.

On his last visit to Sydney, Stevenson sat for an unknown sculptor, deeming the result to be 'an excellent likeness of Mark Twain'. He wrote to Colvin:

> I found my fame much grown on this return to civilisation. *Digito monstrari* is a new experience; people all looked at me in the streets in Sydney; and it was very queer.

On the pavement of the Writers' Walk in Circular Quay, there is set a plaque commemorating his visit: 'renowned poet, novelist and essayist, Scottish-born Robert Louis Stevenson came to Sydney from his home in Samoa (where he was known as Tusitala, 'Teller of Tales') four times in the early 1890s.' No doubt he enjoyed many aspects of his Sydney fame, even if he did not particularly like seeing his face in the newspapers.

> The pictures they publish of me vary considerably... from the most God-like to the criminal... from the 'man with noble bearing' to the 'bloated boy'... I don't mind what they say.

A new detachment is evident in that last remark. The Stevenson quartet left Sydney on 20 March. He wrote in his diary:

> Poor Fanny had very little fun on her visit, having been for most of the time on a diet of maltine and slops... but Belle and I had some lively sport all through...

Fanny had spent much of the time in Sydney depressed and ill in her hotel room and Belle had been Stevenson's regular companion. Their relationship was friendly and relaxed and she partnered him at a Government House reception where he renewed his acquaintanceship with Lady Jersey. Fanny did not attend. Stevenson was in extrovert mood, sporting velvet jacket and red cummerbund. They were photographed together – he and Belle must have made a striking couple.

Lady Jersey later said of him, 'he was not only a writer of romance, but a hero of romance'. Did she perhaps know something about Louis and Belle that we do not?

Everything seemed set fair for Stevenson as he voyaged home, this time, to his own place – built and fully paid for. His family was around him, his name secured for posterity on the spines of books and with the likelihood of all the years of maturity ahead, he should have been happy. But he wrote to Colvin: '…from SS *Mariposa* at sea. Apia due by daybreak tomorrow. Bad pen, bad ink, bad light, bad blotting paper.' Just a bad day perhaps? It was time to take stock. How did he see himself?

> Really knows a good deal… but you could talk a week to him and never guess it… Name in family, The Tame Celebrity. Cigarettes without intermission except when coughing or kissing. Hopelessly entangled in apron-strings. Drinks plenty. Curses some. Temper unstable. Manners purple in emergency… Has been an invalid for years but can boldly claim you can't tell.

He had made it.

> To confess plainly… I can still, looking back, see myself in many favourite attitudes; signalling for a boat from my pirate ship with a pocket handkerchief, I at the jetty end, and one or two of my bold blades keeping the crowd at bay; or else

turning in the saddle to look back on my whole command (some five thousand strong) following me at the hand-gallop up the road out of the burning valley... *Et point du tout*. I am a poor scribe... with neither health nor vice for anything more spirited than procrastination, which I may well call the Consolation Stakes of Wickedness.

Even though he still looked frail, to those who knew him well he now looked better than ever before, but he must have been sorely tried by Fanny's behaviour. He gave her a lot of leeway but, to borrow a phrase from another biographer, Frank McLynn, he was no 'hen-pecked inadequate'. He laid out his domestic parameters and guarded them closely. However, Mr King, who had left Vailima after only a few months, commented 'the women were too much for any man'. Before his departure, he had bearded Stevenson in his den, even though it was forbidden to disturb him there. Stevenson heard out his complaints, then laid down his pen, leaned back in his chair and put his hands behind his head. 'Well, King, you know what women are!' he said. Then, leaning forward again, he added quietly, 'No, by Jove! How can you? Show me the man who does.' Stevenson's own way of dealing with his trio was to *seem* to keep his head in the sand. Avoiding confrontation should not be mistaken for weakness. Besides, he needed all his stamina to deal with the work at hand. He was becoming reliant on Belle:

She runs me like a baby in a perambulator – sees I'm properly dressed; bought me silk socks and sees that I wear them; takes care of me when I'm sick, and I don't know what the devil she doesn't do for me when I'm well from writing my books to trimming my nails. Has a growing conviction that she is the author of my works.

Most of his letters were dictated to Belle, whose face he would have studied as he laced his remarks with teasing ambiguity. Their working relationship involved a necessary intimacy. Belle had become an active witness to his artistic process.

> I sit here and smoke and write, and re-write, and destroy and rage
> at my own impotence, from six in the morning till eight at night,
> with trifling and not always agreeable intervals for meals.

They dealt with mountains of fan mail, but he refused to acknowledge any letter addressed to Robert Louis Stephenson: taking the misspelling as an affront to family honour. One such missive read:

> Dear Mr Stephenson: I've read all your works. I think you
> are the greatest author living. Please send me a complete set
> of Samoan stamps.

Belle had the job of weeding through the hundreds of letters that arrived on each mail ship, extracting the many warm letters from friends like Gosse, and Low, pompous ones from Colvin and what she called 'sailor-like' letters from Henley. There were serious screeds from Bob Stevenson that seemed to worry RLS and letters from Baxter that made him laugh. Baxter always added a little bit in Scotch after his business. Belle liked that, and Stevenson enjoyed replying in the same vein.

Everything was feasible for him now, as long as his lungs held. But let him lose his flair, or his nerve, and the whole thing could come tumbling down about his ears. Meantime, he could enjoy it:

> My house is a great place; we have a hall fifty feet long with
> a great redwood stair ascending from it, where we dine in
> state – on fish usually, if we're lucky; myself usually dressed
> in a singlet and a pair of trousers – attended by servants in
> their *lavalavas* – a kind of kilt, also with flowers in their hair,
> or powdered with lime. The Europeans who come think it
> is a kind of dream.

Not only the Europeans, but the Americans and the Australians. Not a week passed but a journalist turned up at his door. If he saw one coming, Stevenson would retreat to his mother's bedroom but often he was caught, occasionally quite willingly. Marie Fraser, an actress turned journalist, captivated him in every sense. Her interview was published in the *Illustrated London News*. She enquired why his study was in such disorder: 'Things are more easily found when they are left lying about,' he said.

At this stage of her life, Fanny seemed to be permanently on the verge of hysteria, obsessed with hypochondriacal imagining that she was dying. Stevenson was almost convinced that she was going mad.

It did not help matters that Lloyd's sexual relationship with a Samoan girl was causing some embarrassment. In addition to other revelations, Stevenson finally awoke to what a selfish ingrate his stepson was. How lucky then, that his stepdaughter was proving to be a true ally.

Thanks to her, he continued to write throughout the many distractions, and write well. *The Ebb-Tide* would be finished by June, though he had to resort completely to dictation due to severe attacks of cramp in his right hand – what is termed today Repetitive Strain Injury. He called it 'scrivener's palsy'. Notwithstanding, the Vailima production line never halted. Day after day the words poured out of him and into Belle's notebook.

> As long as the pen will scratch and the words will come I see no reason to blame God or the solar system for any little irritation I may cause myself... Here are, indeed, labours for a Hercules in a dress coat, armed with a pen and a dictionary... to paint the portrait of the insufferable sun...

How does any artist rate his achievements? Stevenson never regarded his writing as high art:

> I wonder if I've done anything at all good; and who can tell

me? And why should I wish to know? In so little a while, I, and the English language, and the bones of my descendants, will have ceased to be a memory!

But the artist in him could not be denied: 'And yet – and yet – one would like to leave an image for a few years upon men's minds – for fun.' But the creator of Mr Hyde had his own shadow.

For fourteen years I have not had a day's real health and yet with not a hope of my dying soon and cleanly, and 'winning off the stage'. If I could die just now, or say in half a year, I should have had a splendid time of it on the whole. But it gets a little stale, and my work will begin to senesce and people start to shy bricks at me... I was meant to die young, but the Gods do not love me. And now it looks as if I should survive to see myself impotent and forgotten. It's a pity suicide is not thought the ticket in the best circles.

In building Vailima, he had not gone for the easy option. He could have lived a life of leisure on The Beach with the rest of the expatriates. The house continually drained his considerable earnings and left him worrying about cash flow, even though every word he sold between 1891 and 1893 had a price tag on it of roughly a dollar. Whatever the payment, he could never get enough of writing. It was his drug, his medicine, his sustainer. Reading his best work today, one can feel the relish he had for the task, especially when dealing in dialogue, particularly Scots dialogue. Every single day something had to be set down. Even so, it was by no means all work and no play. Graham Balfour, his chess opponent and tennis adversary ('He's the same kind of fool we are!'), accompanied him on a trip to Hawaii after *The Ebb-Tide* had been completed. After nearly a year, the time had come for the cousins to part – Graham planned to travel on through Melanesia.

Stevenson's valet, Ta'alolo, caught measles as soon as they landed in Honolulu. While he was in quarantine, Stevenson addressed the

Thistle Club on the topic of 'Scottish History' – 'which is nothing but one long brawl'. He talked extempore and the speech was very well received. He was made an Honorary Member of the Club.

We know now how little time he had left, but as long as Belle's fingers could keep pace with the pictures in his head, the mountains of letters, and the ongoing demands of publishers and editors, he saw no reason to fret about the Universe. He lived in the Multiverse of his own mind.

He was now working on two books, *St Ives* and *The Justice Clerk* (later titled *Weir of Hermiston*).

I think if I'd written nothing more than *Kidnapped* and 'Thrawn Janet' I would be worthy of a place among men of letters... but this *Hermiston* will be the best thing I've done, I think. I have in mind a scene for it where Kirstie comes to her lover in prison and confesses that she is with child by the man he has murdered. It will be the strongest scene in the book, the finest I have written... Yes, Kirstie. I feel her growing in me till I am almost in love with her, smart in her Glasgow braws... I must finish it...

Stevenson dedicated the book to Fanny:

I saw rain falling and a rainbow drawn on Lammermuir.
Hearkening, I heard again in my precipitous city,
Beaten bells winnow the keen, sea wind.
And here afar, intent on my own race and place, I wrote.
Take thou the writing, thine it is.
For who burnished the coals,
Held still the target higher,
Chary of praise and prodigal of counsel,
Who, but thou?
And now, in the end, if this the least be good,
If any fire burn in the imperfect page,
The praise be thine.

Though there is no doubting the sincerity of this charming enco-mium, it hardly reflects the reality of their relationship in the final Vailima years.

> [Fanny] runs the show. Infinitely little, extraordinary wig of grey curls, handsome waxen face like Napoleon's, insane black eyes, boy's hands, tiny bare feet, a cigarette, wild blue native dress usually spotted with garden mould... Hellish energy relieved by fortnights of entire hibernation. Can make anything from a house to a row, all fine and large of their kind. Doctors everything... cannot be doctored herself... vio-lent friend, a brimstone enemy... either loathed or slavishly adored... dreams dreams and sees visions.

It seems that Fanny's life-role had been undermined by her husband's upsurge in vitality. At the age of fifty-four, her spiky temperament was sharper than ever and for Stevenson, the husband became a more difficult part to play than the writer. The 'tiger lily of the bed' had become the snarling lioness of the separate bedroom. The combination of manic depression and menopausal mood-swings made her demonic and the servants ran away in real fear at her wild rages. In the Garden of Eden which she had worked so hard to create, Eve had become the serpent. Harry Moors, never a friend to Fanny, offered Stevenson the use of his place on Nassau Island as a bolt-hole, but Stevenson declined, preferring to retreat to his den and lose himself in Flaubert.

In the library each morning, there was Belle, notebook on her knee, typewriter at the ready, 'a creature of equal, if unlike frail-ties, whose weak, human heart beats no more tunefully than my own'.

On 13 November, his forty-fourth birthday, carriages streamed up the 'Road of the Loving Heart', which had been built by twenty-seven freed Samoan prisoners as a mark of gratitude to Stevenson for his support during the troubles. It ran from the *Ala Sopo* (the main road from Apia), up to Vailima, a distance of about a quarter of a mile. Forty-four couples had been invited to attend the first Vailima Ball.

> I am now very dandy; I announced two years ago that I should change. Slovenly youth, all right – not slovenly age. So really now I'm pretty spruce; always a white shirt, white neck-tie, fresh shave, silk socks – O, a great sight!

He was in his performing element, the centre of attention, exuding an inextinguishable boyish enthusiasm. The naval band from HMS *Katoomba* struck up and he danced with Belle till two in the morning. He who had so often walked arm-in-arm with Death now linked arms with Life and danced the night away with joyous abandon.

It is the business of this life to make
excuses for others, but none for ourselves.
ETHICAL STUDIES

Postscript

Let us say only goodnight.
The shadows are already closing in
and it gets dark for all of us...

I

I HAVE THOUGHT myself so vividly into the life of Robert Louis Stevenson that he lives in my imagination like an old friend. From the chill and smoke of Edinburgh to the sophisticated literary haunts of London, from the canals of France to the glaciers of Switzerland, from California to Sydney and finally to torrid Samoa – I see and understand all these places as if through his eyes. I first set foot in Apia on 1 December 1994. I was there as a guest of the Western Samoan Robert Louis Stevenson Centenary Committee. I had been invited with Stevenson enthusiasts from all over the world to commemorate the centenary of the death of Tusitala, and so here I was at the end of the trail.

In 1897 Fanny had virtually given Vailima away – to a wood merchant who sold it to the German Government, exactly what Stevenson would not have wanted. From 1919 to 1962 Vailima was administered by the New Zealand Government. It then lay derelict for many years, buffeted by all the winds that mightily blow in the South Pacific, until it was rescued by two American Mormon missionaries and restored to something of its former self in time for the Stevenson Centenary.

I stood alone on the verandah and looked out to sea, as Stevenson must have done a hundred years before, almost to the day. In my mind's eye, there are stored so many indelible images of his last hours: the dawn breaking as he smoked his first cigarette of the day; the next chapter of *Weir of Hermiston* taking a grip of him; an intense session dictating to Belle. She remembers: 'He had hardly more than a line or two to keep him on track, but never falters for a word, giving me sentences with capital letters and full stops as easily and steadily as if he were reading from an unseen book. He walks up and down as I write and his voice is so beautiful, and the story so interesting, that I forget the rest.' Then, early in the evening, after a bathe in the waterfall pool, he made his last descent of the grand staircase to help Fanny prepare dinner. As he tossed a salad, he suddenly dropped the spoons and raised his fingers to his temples. 'Do I look strange?' he asked. These were his last words, for he dropped to the floor at her feet.

In a sense, Stevenson could not have made a better exit. What could be better than to depart this world at the very peak of potential? With *Weir of Hermiston* he achieved an unprecedented level of complexity and depth. He was at the threshold of a new cycle of creativity.

In the famous photograph of Louis and Belle working together, there is something about their body language that arrests the eye. Stevenson leans back on a chair, elegant as ever. He is looking away from Belle and towards the camera. She is seated, attentively transcribing. In that frozen moment I read something else, something that would never be said out loud. Belle and Louis had grown closer than either of them wanted to acknowledge. One can imagine their eyes meeting, expressing the unspoken awareness that, in their hearts, they were indeed lovers. He had suddenly seen 'the face of woman as she was' and he had died as he had wanted: 'in the hot fit of life, a tip-toe on the highest point, he passes at a bound to the other side– trailing with him his clouds of glory, this happy-starred, full-blooded spirit shoots into the spiritual land'. RLS died in an exquisitely unfulfilled moment.

Tafaie, my driver, waited in the car. She wouldn't get out. She said that Vailima was haunted and that some of her friends had seen Tusitala smoking late at night. I would have given anything to see him – even as a ghost. I would have loved to wander with him through his preposterous wooden castle.

Now I was walking down the very stairs he had walked down, passing through the very doors he had passed through, sitting at the very table where he had sat. I stood in the library – and I felt nothing. I couldn't feel his presence – hear his voice: 'I do think this will be confoundedly good, Belle.'

Stevenson's colossal industry created Vailima, but the colossus of his reputation made it what it is now – a sentimental mausoleum. Thousands of visitors traipse through the Stevenson Museum Gift Shop every year. But there were no cruise ship tourists on the day I was there. I was on my own, looking for a ghost. I let myself out through the back door. I was glad that I had come, but sorry that Tusitala was not at home.

The highlight of the Centenary Week was the trek to Stevenson's grave on Mount Vaia. Despite the fact that we had to be up by 4am, several hundred people assembled at the gates of Vailima. They stood in the darkness, holding candles, trying to keep them alight as the first drops of rain fell. A Samoan Catholic priest said a few words I couldn't hear, and the combined college choirs sang the 'Requiem'.

> Under the wide and starry sky
> Dig the grave and let me lie,
> Glad did I live and gladly die
> And I laid me down with a will...

Only they sang it in Samoan:

> I lalo o le lagi ma fe tu eli ai lou
> Tuugamau ou te taoto fiafia
> Ou te taoto saunia...

The warm Samoan rain was now falling steadily. I thought, 'God's crying'. Crying for our Scotch Tusitala. I stood there under a little tartan umbrella, marvelling at what Stevenson had attained.

At the end of the song we moved off. For some reason, my heart was pounding with excitement. This was it. This was what I had come to Samoa for – to ascend Mount Vaea by way of 'The Road of the Loving Heart' and stand at Stevenson's tomb. It was to be the climax of the quest for me.

Day was breaking as we reached the clearing under the summit. We had made it. The gravestone was an uncompromising slab of white concrete. I bent to read the inscription:

This be the verse you grave for me
Here he lies where he longed to be...

Among the blooms that festooned the plinth was a sprig of heather.

Home is the sailor, home from sea
And the hunter home from the hill.

A conch shell sounded. It was time for me to speak.

You, who pass this grave, put aside hatred, love kindness, be all services remembered in your heart, and all offence pardoned...

The syllables floated in the air like petals.

Here may the winds about me blow
Here the clouds may come and go,
Here shall he rest for evermo'
And the heart for ay shall be still.

The choir gently hummed their setting of 'Requiem', bringing a melodic counterpoint to the lines. In the silence that followed, we all stood with heads bowed, each with their own thoughts of Stevenson, his death, his life. When I spoke again, it was almost in a whisper.

The morning is such a morning as you have never seen; heaven upon earth for sweetness, depth upon depth of unimaginable colour and huge silence broken at this moment only by the far-away murmur of the Pacific – and the rich piping of a single bird.

An Australian piper stationed on the slopes far below started to play 'The Floo'ers o' the Forest'. For a precious moment, there was magic in the air. As if on cue, a bird rose high in the air in a cascade of song. You can't teach God anything about stage-management.

2

The Vailima household broke up almost as soon as the magnet-core had gone. With Stevenson's death, Fanny enjoyed a new lease of life. She received hundreds of letters of sympathy. Her old friend Henry James wrote:

To have lived in the light of that splendid life, that beautiful, bountiful being – only to see it from one moment to the other converted into a fable as strange and romantic as one of his own... He lighted up one whole side of the globe, and was in himself a whole province of one's imagination... He has gone in time not to be old, early enough to be generously young and late enough to have drunk deep of the cup.

Charles Baxter was on his way to Samoa when the grim news reached him. Stevenson had been canny enough to put the title to Vailima in Baxter's name, in case of any fallout from his political involvement locally. On his arrival in Samoa, Baxter, like the gentleman he was, immediately signed the house over to Fanny – together with Stevenson's Scottish Bar pension, the rights to his literary estate, and full royalties. Like the lady she was, Fanny took it all with both hands, and then coolly showed Baxter the door.

She outlived her husband by almost twenty years, living the life of the archetypal merry widow. She made decisions lightly and quickly, and mostly wrongly, on virtually every aspect of the Stevenson estate. Destructive on all fronts, she managed to ruin her son's marriage to Katharine Durham, a spirited woman who gave as good as she got until the spineless Lloyd chose his mother over her. He eventually remarried and drifted to New York. For a man who had no talents of his own, he had done very well indeed.

Fanny took as her lover 'companion' a young playwright, Ned Field, who was the same age as her grandson. At her death in 1914, despite her prodigal lifestyle, she had more than a hundred thousand dollars in the bank.

And now for a remarkable turn of events. Belle, who had settled in Wellington, New Zealand, herself married Ned Field shortly after Fanny's death. Both Ned and and her son Austin became successful playwrights. In 1936 oil was found on land that Ned owned, and he promptly died – of shock, no doubt – leaving Belle a millionairess in her own right. She was to be the last survivor of the Vailima household. She died in her nineties in 1953, and with her died the Stevenson story we shall never know.

Asked by Colvin if she knew what RLS had in mind for *Weir of Hermiston*, Belle said she was sure he had 'some dramatic destiny' for Kirstie. It is my own view that Louis had some dramatic destiny in mind for Belle – but we'd better let that flea stick to the wa'.

*I was not born for age... you can
never write a better dedication to the
vanished...Tusitala*
LAST LETTER TO EDMUND GOSSE

RLS: A Concise Chronology

Passion, wisdom, creative force, the power of mystery or colour, are allotted in the hour of birth, and can neither be learned nor simulated.
ETHICAL STUDIES

1850 Born on 13 November at 8 Howard Place, Edinburgh, to Margaret and Thomas Stevenson.

1852 Alison Cunningham ('Cummy') joins household as nurse to infant Louis.

1853 Family moves to 1 (now 9) Inverleith Terrace.

1854 Stories to this date dictated to Cummy, but destroyed, unpublished.

1856 First-ever writing, *A History of Moses* co-written with his mother. Privately printed for A Edward Newton, 1919.

1857 Family moves to 17 Heriot Row.
Sporadic attendance at Infant School in Canonmills.

1858 Morning tuition at Robert Henderson's Special School in India Street.

1859 *The American Travellers* dictated to Aunt Jane Whyte Balfour during visit to Colinton Manse. (MS Anderson 1914. Unpublished).
The Book of Joseph dictated to his mother.
Travels in Perthshire – written on holiday at Bridge of Allan; mentions trips to Dundee and Crieff. Dictated to mother with own drawings. (MS Anderson 1014).

1861 Enrols at Edinburgh Academy.
Continues to write 'pleasant and diverse narratives', such as *The Adventures of Basil* (in the style of Captain Mayne-Reid), at home and at Colinton Manse, with the help of various amanuenses.
The Antiquities of Midlothian dictated to his mother. (MS Yale. Unpublished.)

1863 Transfers to Mr Thomson's School 'for backward and delicate boys' in Frederick Street.
Travels with parents and Cummy to South of France; Italy as far south as Naples, returning via Rome, Florence and Venice; returns via the Brenner Pass, through into Austria and Germany.

1864 Attends Burlington Lodge Academy at Spring Grove, Isleworth,

Middlesex for the autumn term.

First letters in French.

Contributes stories to Issue No. 1 of *The Schoolboy's Magazine*.

Visits London, where he stays at the Craven Hotel, with his father.

Christmas at Menton.

1865   Summer holiday in Peebles.

Writes holiday essay: 'I tried to do justice to the inhabitants... in the style of *The Book of Snobs*.'

The Baneful Potato (Libretto for an opera, now lost).

The Plague Seller with cousin, Henrietta Traquair. (Unpublished. Photostat Yale.)

First draft outline of *Deacon Brodie*, a play.

At Torquay with mother.

Co-edits *The Trial* magazine.

1866   Contributes various stories to *The Sunbeam* magazine, including 'The Banker's Ward'.

Writes *The Pentland Rising*, a sixteen-page pamphlet; 100 copies printed by Andrew Elliott, Edinburgh, and distributed privately by Thomas Stevenson. MS untraced.

1867   Bridge of Allan.

Family acquires Swanston Cottage as holiday home. At North Berwick with father.

Enters Edinburgh University in the Faculty of Engineering.

During Natural Philosophy lecture by PG Tait lists plays he would like to write.

1868   Visits Wick and Anstruther with father. Stays at Cunzie House. Writes 'Night Outside the Wick Mail', a narrative of the journey: unpublished. *Monmouth: A Tragedy*, begun with cousin, RM Stevenson, but completed alone.

1869   To Orkney and Shetland Islands on the *Pharos* with father.

Keeps journal of voyage.

Elected as member of the Speculative Society at Edinburgh University. Contributes papers

'Painting and Words', an essay – unpublished.

Cosmo, a novel. Unfinished.

A Covenanting Story-Book. Unpublished. MS at Haverford College Library, Yale.

1870   To the Isle of Earraid with father. Meets Edmond Gosse, Sam Bough. Visits his cousin, Maud Wilson, at Cockfield Rectory, Suffolk, where she is the wife of the rector, the Revd Churchill Babbington. Fined for 'snow-balling' in the Edinburgh streets.

1871 Joins Fleeming and Annie Jenkin's amateur theatrical troupe.

Awarded the Silver Medal of the Edinburgh Society of Arts for his paper, 'Notice of a New Form of Intermittent Light for Lighthouses', but transfers from Engineering Faculty to Law. Writes for Edinburgh University magazine.

Joins Edinburgh firm of solicitors, WF Skene and Peacock, as legal trainee.

Keeps private journal as law clerk.

1872 Visits Bridge of Allan and Dunblane.

Holidays in Germany with Walter Simpson.

Founds the L(iberty)J(ustice)R(everence) Club with cousin Bob Stevenson and others.

Passes preliminary examination for the Scottish Bar.

1873 Reads paper on 'The Thermal Influence of Forests' at a meeting of the Royal Society of Edinburgh.

Visits Malvern. Re-visits his cousin, Maud, at Cockfield Rectory.

Meets Fanny Sitwell and Sidney Colvin.

In London, Dr Andrew Clark recommends returning to the South of France.

Denied try for the English Bar.

Writes autobiographical reminiscences as basis for 'Memoirs of Himself' (1880) and 'Rosa Quo Locorum' (1893).

'Roads' accepted by Mr Hammerton for *Portfolio* magazine. This earns him his first writing fee.

1874 Spring at Menton.

Stays with Colvin at Hampstead.

Elected to the Savile Club. Meets Edmund Gosse.

Cruises with Walter Simpson through the Inner Hebrides.

Resumes law classes.

Christmas at Cambridge with Colvin.

Two more articles for *Portfolio*: 'Notes on the Movements of Young Children' and 'On the Enjoyment of Unpleasant Places'. Receives five pounds for 'Ordered South', published by *Macmillan's Magazine*.

1875 Plays the Duke, Orsino, in *Twelfth Night*.

Meets WE Henley at Edinburgh Royal Infirmary.

Called to the Scottish Bar.

Returns to France.

Visits Barbizon with Bob Stevenson.

Essay on Burns rejected by *Encyclopaedia Britannica* but is paid five guineas for it. (Reworks the material for 'Some Aspects of Robert Burns' in 1879).

'The Charity Bazaar' (sketch).

'Appeal to the Clergy of the Church of Scotland' (essay).

1876   Walking tour through Ayrshire and Galloway. Reviews Salvini's *Macbeth*.

West Highlands with the Jenkins.

Spring in London.

Summer on canoe trip through French canals with Walter Simpson.

Visits Grez-sur-Loing with cousin, Bob Stevenson. Joins the artistic colony at Barbizon. Meets Fanny Osbourne.

'A Winter's Walk in Carrick and Galloway'. Unfinished, but published by Cooper Hay, Glasgow, 1999.

1877   London, before joining Fanny Osbourne in Paris.

'Lodging for the Night' in October issue of *Temple Bar* magazine. First short story to be published.

1878   Secretary to Fleeming Jenkin at the Paris Exposition.

Fanny returns to America.

'Crabbed Age and Youth' published in *Cornhill* magazine.

Walking tour in the Cévennes.

An Inland Voyage – his first book, based on holiday with Simpson in 1876, is published by Kegan Paul, London.

1879   Works on *Deacon Brodie* (a play) with WE Henley.

In London for publication of second book, *Travels with a Donkey in the Cévennes*. (Kegan Paul, London).

After receiving a cable from Fanny in America, sails from Greenock for New York on the *Devonia*.

Travels by train to California.

Arrives in Monterey and re-unites with Fanny and family. Contributes to the *Monterey Californian*.

Fanny moves back to husband, Sam Osbourne, in Oakland. Louis follows and proposes. She accepts, leaves husband and moves with son, Samuel Lloyd Osbourne, to join Louis in San Francisco.

'Pavilion on the Links' published in *Cornhill* magazine.

Edinburgh: Picturesque Notes (Seeley, Jackson and Halliday, London).

1880   Marriage in San Francisco on 19 May. Honeymoon at Silverado, Napa County.

Sails on *City of Chester* for Liverpool with wife and step-son.

Returns to Edinburgh.

Goes on Highland holiday with family to Strathpeffer.

Re-works *Deacon Brodie* with WE Henley.

Attends Dr Karl Reudi's clinic at Davos, Switzerland.

Meets JA Symonds in Davos.

1881 London.
Returns to Davos.
Holidays at Pitlochry and Braemar.
Works on 'Not I' and other poems.
Book of essays, *Virginibus Puerisque*, published by Kegan Paul.

1882 Davos again. Returns to London.
Edinburgh. Peebles. Kingussie.
South of France with Bob Stevenson. Rejoins Fanny in Marseilles. They move into Campagne Defli, San Marcel.
First performance of *Deacon Brodie* at Bradford.
Familiar Studies of Men and Books (Chatto and Windus, London).
Moral Emblems (privately printed by Lloyd Osbourne, Davos Press at Davos).
The New Arabian Nights (Chatto and Windus, London).

1883 La Solitude, Hyères. Royat.
The Silverado Squatters (Chatto and Windus, London).
Treasure Island published by Cassell and Company, London, following serialisation in *Young Folks*.

1884 Visited by Baxter and Henley at Hyères. Excursions to Nice. Outbreak of cholera at Hyères. Returns to London.
Moves to Bonallie Towers, Branksome Park, Bournemouth.
Playwriting sessions with Henley on *Admiral Guinea* and *Beau Austin*.

1885 Moves house to Skerryvore in Alum Chine Road, Bournemouth. Meets Henry James.
Macaire, a re-working of old melodrama with Henley.
Visits Thomas Hardy in Dorchester.
Ill in Exeter. In Bournemouth is treated by Dr Thomas Bodley Scott.
A Child's Garden of Verses – adapted from the original *Penny Whistles* (1883) published by Chatto and Windus.
More Arabian Nights/The Dynamiter (Chatto and Windus. *Prince Otto: A Romance* (Chatto and Windus), dramatised by Gerald Gurney for theatre production in Britain.

1886 In London with Colvin.
Strange Case of Dr Jekyll and Mr Hyde (Longmans, Green, London).
Kidnapped (Cassell and Company, after serial publication in *Young Folks*).
Holiday in Paris with Fanny.

1887 Thomas Stevenson dies in Edinburgh. on 8 May.
'Thomas Stevenson – Engineer' published in *Contemporary Review*.

Family sail to New York, with Mrs Stevenson.

Newport, Rhode Island.

Settles at Saranac. Treated by Dr EL Trudeau.

'Memoir of Fleeming Jenkin' for *Nature* magazine.

The Hanging Judge (play) co-written with Fanny. (This was privately printed by Thomas J Wise in 1914 with an Introduction by Edmund Gosse.)

Memories and Portraits (Chatto and Windus).

The Merry Men (Chatto and Windus).

Underwoods (Scribner's).

'Ticonderoga' (poem) in *Scribner's Magazine*, December issue.

1888 New York City.

Family leaves for California.

'Nixie' quarrel with Henley by letter.

Manasquan, New Jersey. New York. Joins Fanny and family in San Francisco.

Sets out on first South Seas voyage on the *Casco* under Captain Otis. Sees the Marquesas, Paumotus, the Society Islands, and the Sandwich Islands.

'A Chapter on Dreams' and 'The Lantern-Bearers' in issues of *Scribner's Magazine*.

The Black Arrow: A Tale of the Two Roses (Scribner's).

'The Misadventure of John Nicholson'. A Christmas story. (Cassell and Company).

1889 Lands at Honolulu in Hawaii.

Sails in the *Equator* for the Gilbert Islands.

First sight of Samoa.

Buys land at Upolu through Harry J Moors, an American trader.

The Master of Ballantrae (Scribner's; Serialised the previous year in *Scribner's Magazine*).

The Wrong Box, co-written with Lloyd Osbourne. (Scribner's).

1890 Sydney, Australia.

On *Janet Nicholl* to Gilbert and Marshall Islands. Stays in Noumea.

Father Damien. (*Open Letter to Mr Hyde of Honolulu*). Edition of twenty-five copies printed in Sydney.

In the South Seas (Cassell and Company).

1891 Sails to Sydney to meet mother arriving from Scotland.

'The Bottle Imp'– a short story published in missionary newspaper in Samoan language.

1892 Building of Vailima.

Treated by Dr Funk.

Across the Plains (Chatto and Windus).

The Beach of Falesà (Twenty-five copies printed by Cassell for copyright). *A Footnote to History* (Cassell and Company).

The Wrecker co-written with Lloyd Osbourne serialised in *Scribner's Magazine* and novel published by Scribner's.

1893   Vailima completed.

Civil war in Samoa.

Travels to Honolulu.

Catriona serialised in *News of the World* as *David Balfour*. Later published in book form by Cassell and Company.

Island Nights' Entertainments (Cassell and Company).

1894   Samoan chiefs build 'Road of the Loving Heart' as gesture of thanks to Stevenson.

Feast at Vailima for forty-fourth birthday.

The Ebb-Tide, begun by Lloyd Osbourne and completed by Stevenson, serialised in thirteen parts for *McClure's* magazine. Published in book form by William Heinemann, London).

Abandons *St Ives* to begin *Weir of Hermiston*, dictating it to Isobel Strong. Dies of cerebral haemorrhage on the porch at Vailima, 3 December 1894.

Buried on Mt Vaea the next day.

Bibliography

*Every generation has to educate another
which it has brought upon the stage.*
ETHICAL STUDIES

Aldington, Richard — *Portrait of a Rebel*, London, 1957

Balfour, Graham — *The Life of Robert Louis Stevenson*, London, 1901

Barrie, JM — *An Edinburgh Eleven*, London, 1889

Bathurst, Bella — *The Lighthouse Stevensons*, London, 1999

Bell, Gavin — *In Search of Tusitala*, London, 1994

Bell, Ian — *Dreams of Exile*, Edinburgh, 1992

Bevan, Brian — *RLS: Poet and Teller of Tales*, London, 1994

Bok, Edward W.

Booth, Bradford and Ernest Mehew (eds) — *The Playful Stevenson*, New York, 1927

Cairney, John — *The Letters of Robert Louis Stevenson*, New Haven, 1994–95

Mr RLS (a solo play), Solsgirth, 1973

— *Mr and Mrs RLS* (a duologue), St Andrews, 1979

— *A Scotch Tusitala* (a play for radio), Radio New Zealand 1993

The Theatricality of RLS (Thesis) Victoria University, NZ, 1994

Calder, Jenni — *RLS: A Life Study*, London, 1980

Calder, Jenni (ed) — *The Robert Louis Stevenson Companion*, Edinburgh, 1980

— *Stevenson and Victorian Scotland*, Edinburgh, 1981

— *RLS: A Critical Celebration*, Edinburgh, 1987

Caldwell, Elsie — *Last Witness for Robert Louis Stevenson*, Norman, 1960

Campbell, Ian (ed) — *Selected Short Stories of RLS*, Edinburgh, 1980

Carmen, Bliss — *A Threnody for RLS*, Boston, 1895

Carothers, Alva — *Stevenson's Isles of Paradise*, Santa Barbara, 1931

Chesterton, Gilbert Keith — *RLS*, London, 1927

Clarke, W	'RLS in Samoa', *Yale Review*, Yale, 1921
Colvin, Sidney	*Memories and Notes of Persons and Places 1852–1912*, London, 1921
	— *Robert Louis Stevenson: Man and Writer*, London, 1924
Colvin, Sidney (ed)	*The Letters of Robert Louis Stevenson*, London, 1911
Cookson, Gillian and Hempstead, Colin A	*A Victorian Scientist and Engineer: Fleeming Jenkin and the Birth of Electrical Engineering*, Aldershot, 2000
Cooper, Lettice	*Robert Louis Stevenson*, London, 1947
Cope-Cornford, Leslie	*The Life of Robert Louis Stevenson*, London, 1899
Cowell, Henry J	*Robert Louis Stevenson*, London, 1945
Cruse, Amy	*Robert Louis Stevenson*, London, 1915
Daiches, David	*Robert Louis Stevenson* Glasgow, 1947
	— *Stevenson and the Art of Fiction*, New York, 1951
	— *Robert Louis Stevenson and his World*, London, 1973
Davies, Hunter	*The Teller of Tales*, London, 1994
Day, A Grove (ed)	*Travels in Hawaii*, Hawaii, 1973
Eaton Charlotte	'Stevenson at Manasquan', *Queen's Quarterly*, 1931
Eigner, Edwin	*Robert Louis Stevenson and the Romantic Tradition*, Princeton, 1966
Ellison, Joseph W	*Tusitala of the South Seas*, New York, 1953
Elwin, Malcolm	*The Strange Case of RLS*, London 1950
	—*The Essays of RLS*, London, 1950
Ferguson, De Lancey and Waingrow, Marshall (eds)	*Stevenson's Letters to Charles Baxter*, London, 1956
Field, Isobel Osbourne Strong	*Robert Louis Stevenson*, Saranac Lake 1920
Findlay, JP	— *This Life I've Loved*, London, 1937
Findlay, JG	*In the Footsteps of RLS*, Edinburgh n.d.
	Humbugs and Homilies, Christchurch, NZ, 1908
Fitzpatrick, Elayne Wareing	*A Quixotic Companionship*, Monterey, 1994
Fraser, Marie	
Furnas, JC	*In Stevenson's Samoa*, London, 1895
Genung, John F	*Voyage to Windward*, London, 1952

Gibson, John S — *Stevenson's Attitude to Life*, New York, 1901

Gosse, Edmund — *Deacon Brodie: Father to Jekyll and Hyde*, Edinburgh, 1977

'Personal Memories of RLS', *Century*, July 1895.

— *Biographical Notes on the Writings of RLS*, London, 1905

Guthrie, J

— *Critical Kit-Kats*, London, 1913

Hamilton, Clayton — *Some Personal Recollections of the Late Lord Guthrie*, Edinburgh, 1920

Hammerton, JA (ed)

Hampden, John — *On the Trail of Stevenson*, New York, 1916

Hart, James D (ed) — *Stevensonia*, Edinburgh, 1907

The Stevenson Companion, London, 1950

Hellman, George S — *From Scotland to Silverado*, Cambridge Mass, 1966

Issler, Anne Roller

Henley, William Ernest — *The True Stevenson*, Boston, 1925

Johnstone, Arthur — *Stevenson in Colorado*, Caldwell, 1939

'RLS', *Pall Mall*, London, December 1901

Jones, Nigel — *Recollections of Robert Louis Stevenson in the Pacific*, London, 1905

Kelman John

Through a Glass Darkly, New York, 1991

Kerrigan, Catherine (ed) — *The Faith of Robert Louis Stevenson*, Edinburgh, 1903

Kieley, Robert

Weir of Hermiston, Edinburgh, 1995

Knight, Alanna — *RLS and the Fiction of Adventure*, Cambridge, Mass, 1964

The Private Life of RLS (play), Edinburgh, 1973

Knight, Alanna (ed) — *The Passionate Kindness*, Aylesbury, 1974

(co-ed. Warfel, Elizabeth) — *Memoirs of Himself* (unpublished MS)

— *RLS Treasury*, London, 1985

Koiwa, Kumiko — *RLS in the South Seas*, Edinburgh, 1986

— *Robert Louis Stevenson: Bright Ring of Words*, Nairn, 1994

Lang, Andrew — *On the South Sea Island Where You Lie*, Yokohama, 1996

Lapierre, Alexandra — 'Recollections of RLS', *North American Review*, 1899

Low, Will H — *Fanny Stevenson: Muse, Adventuress and*

Lucas, EV — *Romantic Enigma*, London, 1995

Mackay, Margaret — *A Chronicle of Friendships, 1873–1900*, London, 1908

Mackenzie, Compton

McGaw, Sister Martha Mary — *The Colvins and their Friends*, London, 1928

McLaren, Moray

McLynn, Frank — *The Violent Friend*, New York, 1968

Maixner, Paul (ed) — *Robert Louis Stevenson*, London, 1968

Stevenson in Hawaii, Honolulu, 1950

Masson, Rosaline — *Stevenson and Edinburgh*, London, 1950

Robert Louis Stevenson, London, 1993

Masson, Rosaline (ed) — *Robert Louis Stevenson: The Critical Heritage*, London, 1981

Moors, Harry J — *The Life of Robert Louis Stevenson*, Edinburgh, 1923

Mrantz, Maxine

Muir, Edwin — *I Can Remember Robert Louis Stevenson*, Edinburgh, 1922

Nolan, Scott Allen

With Stevenson in Samoa, London, 1910

Osbourne, Lloyd — *Poet in Paradise*, Honolulu, 1977

Pope-Hennessy, James — 'RLS', *Modern Scot*, 1931

Raleigh, Sir Walter — *RLS: Life, Literature and the Silver Screen*, USA, 1993

Rankin, Nicholas

Rice, Edward — *An Intimate Portrait of RLS*, New York, 1924

Rice, Wallace and Frances — *Robert Louis Stevenson*, London, 1974

Ricklefs, Roger (ed) — *RLS*, London, 1895

Dead Man's Chest, London, 1987

Sandison, Alan — *Journey to Upolu*, New York, 1974

The Stevenson Birthday Book, London, 1897

Saposnick, Irving S

Scally, John — *The Mind of Robert Louis Stevenson*, New York, 1962

Simpson, Eve Blantyre

Smith, Janet Adam (Editor) — *Robert Louis Stevenson and the Appearance of Modernism*, London, 1966

Steele, Karen

Stern, Gladys Bronwyn — *Robert Louis Stevenson*, Boston, 1974

Steuart, JA — *Pictures of the Mind*, Edinburgh, 1994

The RLS Originals, Edinburgh, 1912

Stevenson, Fanny Vandegrift — *RLS: Collected Poems*, London, 1950

Stevenson, Margaret — *The Sayings of RLS*, London, 1994

Stevenson, Robert Louis — *Robert Louis Stevenson*, London, 1952

Robert Louis Stevenson, Man and Writer, London, 1924

Stubbs, Laura — *Our Samoan Adventure*, London, 1956

	Letters from Samoa, London, 1906
	— *Works*, Pentland Edition, 1907
	— *Works*, Tusitala Edition, 1924
	— *Works*, Skerryvore Edition, 1926
	Stevenson's Shrine, London, 1903
Swearingen, Roger	*The Prose Writings of Robert Louis Stevenson*, London, 1980
Thompson, John Cargill	*The Laird of Samoa*, Edinburgh, 1994
Veeder, William and Hirsch, Gordon	*Dr Jekyll and Mr Hyde after 100 Years*, Chicago, 1988
Watt, Francis	*RLS*, London, 1913
Woodhead, Richard	*The Strange Case of RL Stevenson*, Edinburgh, 2001

The Writers' Museum and Makars' Court

Located in the 17th century Lady Stair's House, the museum is dedicated to the lives and work of Scotland's great literary figures, particularly Robert Burns (1759-1796), Sir Walter Scott (1771-1832) and Robert Louis Stevenson (1850-1894). The rich collection of manuscripts, first editions and portraits is complemented by a series of personal exhibits including Burns' writing desk and Scott's chessboard and dining table. The Stevenson collection is of international significance.

Other writers, including contemporary authors, are featured in the museum's temporary exhibition programme.

The adjacent Makars' Court, which takes its name from the Scots word for 'poet', is an evolving national literary monument. Inscribed commemorative flagstones celebrate Scottish writers, from the 14th century John Barbour, to Ian Crichton-Smith who died in 1998. New stones are added on a regular basis.

Lady Stair's House
Lady Stair's Close
Lawnmarket
Royal Mile
Tel. 0131 529 4901
www.cac.org.uk

THE WRITERS' MUSEUM

Some other books published by **Luath** Press

Immortal Memories

A compilation of toasts to the Immortal Memory of Robert Burns, as delivered at Burns suppers around the world, together with other orations, verses and addresses 1801–2001, selected and edited with an introduction by John Cairney
1 84282 009 5 HB £20.00

The annual Burns Supper... has become something of a cult in virtually every country in the work where 'Scottish' is spoken – and even where it is not.

Thus begins John Cairney's latest work focusing on Scotland's national bard, Robert Burns. To be asked to deliver the 'Immortal Memory', the chief toast and centrepiece of the traditional Burns Supper, is recognised as a privilege cherished by Burns enthusiasts the world over. *Immortal Memories* is an extensive collection of these toasts, spanning two hundred years from the first Burns Supper in Alloway in 1801 to the Millennium Burns Suppers of 2001.

For over thirty years John Cairney has been regarded as the embodiment of Burns, thanks to his inspired portrayal of the poet in the 1968 Scottish TV production, *Burns*. He has delivered innumerable toasts 'To the Immortal Memory of Robert Burns' and has performed his Burns one-man-show in almost every country in the world.

On the Trail of Robert Burns

John Cairney
0 946487 510 PB £7.99

Is there anything new to say about Robert Burns? John Cairney says it's time to trash Burns the Brand and come on the trail of the real Robert Burns. He is the best of travelling companions on this convivial, entertaining journey to the heart of the Burns story.

Internationally known as 'the face of Robert Burns', John Cairney believes that the traditional Burns tourist trail urgently needs to find a new direction. In an acting career spanning forty years he has often lived and breathed Robert Burns on stage. *On the Trail of Robert Burns* shows just how well he has got under the skin of Burn's complex character. This fascinating journey around Scotland is a rediscovery of Scotlands national bard as a flesh and blood genius. *On the Trail of Robert Burns* outlines five key tours, mainly in Scotland.

'Always a knowledgeable and engaging Burnsian, his personal Burns tour will delight many. Organised chronologically, the trail is expertly, touchingly, and amusingly followed.' THE HERALD

'Popular and highly recommended, both as an on-the-spot guide and a study of Burns.' THE SCOTS MAGA-

The Luath Burns Companion

John Cairney
1 842282 000 1 PB £10.00

Robert Burns was born in a thunderstorm and lived his brief life by flashes of lightning...
So says John Cairney in his introduction. In those flashes Burns' genius revealed itself. *The Luath Burns Companion* is not another 'complete works' but a personal selection by 'The Man Who Played Robert Burns'. This is very much John's book. He talks with an obvious love of Burns and his work, and from a depth of knowledge developed through forty years of study, writing and performance. The *Companion* includes sixty poems, songs and other works, and an essay that explores Burns's life and influences, his triumphs and tragedies.

Edinburgh's Historic Mile

Duncan Priddle
0 946487 97 9 PB £2.99

This ancient thoroughfare runs downwards and eastwards for just over a mile. Its narrow closes and wynds, each with a distinctive atmosphere and character, have their own stories to tell. From the looming fortress the Castle at the top, to the Renaissance beauty of the palace at the bottom, every step along this ancient highway brings the city's past to life – a past both glorious and gory. Written with all the knowledge and experience the Witchery Tours have gathered in 15 years, it is full of quirky, fun and fascinating stories that you won't find anywhere else. Designed to fit easily in pocket or bag and with a comprehensive map on the back cover this is the perfect book to take on a walk in Edinburgh or read before you arrive.

The Strange Case of RL Stevenson

Richard Woodhead
0 946487 86 3 HB £16.99

A consultant physician for 22 years with a strong interest in Robert Louis Stevenson's life and work, Richard Woodhead was intrigued by the questions raised by the references to his symptoms. The assumption that he suffered from consumption (tuberculosis) – the diagnosis of the day – is challenged in *The Strange Case of RL Stevenson*. Dr Woodhead examines how Stevenson's life was affected by his illness and his perception of it.

This fictional work puts words into the mouths of five doctors who treated RLS at different periods of his adult life. Though these doctors existed in real life, little is documented of their private conversations with RLS. However, everything Dr Woodhead postulates could have occurred within the known framework of RLS's life. RLS's writing continues to compel readers today. The fact that he did much of his writing while confined to his sick-bed is fascinating. What illness could have contributed to his creativity?

'Woodhead's... factual research is faultless, resulting in a good and very readable novel written in the spirit of the time ... a lovely Book at Bedtime.' TIME OUT

'This is a book that can be read in a day and is a real page turner.' BMJ

'I thoroughly enjoyed it. This would make a charming gift for any enthusiastic fan of RLS.' MEDICAL HISTORY JOURNAL

'RLS himself is very much a real figure, as is Fanny, his wife, while his parents are sympathetically and touchingly portrayed.' SCOTS MAGAZINE

THE QUEST FOR

The Quest for the Original Horse Whisperers
Russell Lyon
1 84282 020 6 HB £16.99

The Quest for the Nine Maidens
Stuart McHardy
0 946487 66 9 HB £16.99

The Quest for the Celtic Key
Karen Ralls-MacLeod
& Ian Robertson
1 84282 031 1 PB £8.99

The Quest for Arthur
Stuart McHardy
1 84282 012 5 HB £16.99

ON THE TRAIL OF

On the Trail of John Muir
Cherry Good
0 946487 62 6 PB £7.99

On the Trail of William Wallace
David R Ross
0 946487 47 2 PB £7.99

On the Trail of Robert the Bruce
David R Ross
0 946487 52 9 PB £7.99

On the Trail of Bonnie Prince Charlie
David R Ross
0 946487 68 5 PB £7.99

On the Trail of Mary Queen of Scots
J Keith Cheetham
0 946487 50 2 PB £7.99

On the Trail of Queen Victoria in the
Highlands
Ian R Mitchell
0 946487 79 0 PB £7.99

On the Trail of Robert Service
G Wallace Lockhart
0 946487 24 3 PB £7.99

On the Trail of the Pilgrim Fathers
J Keith Cheetham
0 946487 83 9 PB £7.99

HISTORY

Scots in Canada
Jenni Calder
1 84282 038 9 PB £7.99

Blind Harry's Wallace
Hamilton of Gilbertfield (introduced and edited
by Elspeth King)
0 946487 33 2 PB £8.99

Reportage Scotland: History in the making
Louise Yeoman
0 946487 61 8 PB £9.99

A Word for Scotland
Jack Campbell
0 946487 48 0 PB £12.99

Old Scotland New Scotland
Jeff Fallow
0 946487 40 5 PB £6.99

GENEALOGY

Scottish Roots: Tracing your Scottish ancestors
Alwyn James
1 84282 007 9 PB £9.99

WEDDINGS

The Scottish Wedding Book
G Wallace Lockhart
1 84282 010 9 PB £12.99

FOOD & DRINK

The Whisky Muse: Scotch whisky in poem &
song
collected and introduced by Robin Laing
1 84282 041 9 PB £7.99

LANGUAGE

Luath Scots Language Learner
L Colin Wilson
0 946487 91 X PB £9.99 (book)
1 84282 026 5 £16.99 (double audio CD)

Details of these and other Luath Press titles are available from our website at www.luath.co.uk

Luath Press Limited

committed to publishing well written books worth reading

LUATH PRESS takes its name from Robert Burns, whose little collie Luath (Gael., swift or nimble) tripped up Jean Armour at a wedding and gave him the chance to speak to the woman who was to be his wife and the abiding love of his life. Burns called one of The Twa Dogs Luath after Cuchullin's hunting dog in Ossian's Fingal.

Luath Press was established in 1981 in the heart of Burns country, and is now based a few steps up the road from Burns' first lodgings on Edinburgh's Royal Mile. Luath offers you distinctive writing with a hint of unexpected pleasures.

Most bookshops in the UK, the US, Canada, Australia, New Zealand and parts of Europe, either carry our books in stock or can order them for you. To order direct from us, please send a £sterling cheque, postal order, international money order or your credit card details (number, address of cardholder and expiry date) to us at the address below. Please add post and packing as follows: UK – £1.00 per delivery address; overseas surface mail – £2.50 per delivery address; overseas airmail – £3.50 for the first book to each delivery address, plus £1.00 for each additional book by airmail to the same address. If your order is a gift, we will happily enclose your card or message at no extra charge.

Luath Press Limited
543/2 Castlehill
The Royal Mile
Edinburgh EH1 2ND
Scotland
Telephone: 0131 225 4326 (24 hours)
Fax: 0131 225 4324
email: sales@luath. co.uk
Website: www. luath.co.uk